JOYFUL LiViNG
in the Fourth Dimension

This is a complete list of books by Charles L. Allen since he became a Revell author in 1951.

GOD'S PSYCHIATRY
THE TOUCH OF THE MASTER'S HAND
ALL THINGS ARE POSSIBLE THROUGH PRAYER
WHEN YOU LOSE A LOVED ONE
WHEN THE HEART IS HUNGRY
THE TWENTY-THIRD PSALM
THE TEN COMMANDMENTS
THE LORD'S PRAYER
THE BEATITUDES
TWELVE WAYS TO SOLVE YOUR PROBLEMS
HEALING WORDS
THE LIFE OF CHRIST
PRAYER CHANGES THINGS
THE SERMON ON THE MOUNT
LIFE MORE ABUNDANT
THE CHARLES L. ALLEN TREASURY (with Charles L. Wallis)
ROADS TO RADIANT LIVING
RICHES OF PRAYER
IN QUEST OF GOD'S POWER
WHEN YOU GRADUATE (with Mouzon Biggs)
THE MIRACLE OF LOVE
THE MIRACLE OF HOPE
THE MIRACLE OF THE HOLY SPIRIT
CHRISTMAS IN OUR HEARTS (with Charles L. Wallis)
CANDLE, STAR AND CHRISTMAS TREE (with Charles L. Wallis)
WHEN CHRISTMAS CAME TO BETHLEHEM (with Charles L. Wallis)
CHRISTMAS (with Charles L. Wallis)
WHAT I HAVE LIVED BY
YOU ARE NEVER ALONE
PERFECT PEACE
HOW TO INCREASE YOUR SUNDAY-SCHOOL ATTENDANCE (with Mildred Parker)
THE SECRET OF ABUNDANT LIVING
VICTORY IN THE VALLEYS OF LIFE
FAITH, HOPE, AND LOVE
JOYFUL LIVING

Charles L. Allen

JOYFUL LiViNG in the Fourth Dimension

Fleming H. Revell Company
Old Tappan, New Jersey

Unless otherwise identified Scripture quotations are from the King James Version of the Bible.

Scripture quotations identified RSV are from the Revised Standard Version of the Bible, copyrighted 1946, 1952, © 1971 and 1973.

Quotation from "I'm Waiting for Ships That Never Come In"
Words by Jack Yellen   Music by Abe Olman
Copyright 1919 Forster Music Publisher, Inc. Chicago, Ill. 60604
Copyright Renewal 1947 Forster Music Publisher, Inc.
Used by permission.

Library of Congress Cataloging in Publication Data

Allen, Charles Livingstone, 1913–
    Joyful living in the fourth dimension.

    1. Christian life—Methodist authors.   I. Title.
BV4501.2.A397   1983   248.4'876   82-24136
ISBN 0-8007-1351-6

TO my grandchildren:

Charles L. Allen III
Jack deMange Allen
Margaret Ann Allen
Charles William Miller, Jr.
Carolyn Kay Miller
John O'Brien Miller
John Franklin Allen, Jr.
Benson Haynes Allen
Meredith Ann Allen

Contents

JOYFUL LiViNG
in the Fourth Dimension

ONE
Experiencing the Best of Life

Often people come to me with their problems. I counsel with them and help them seek higher ground. Maybe they face large problems, but they also have a huge potential that hasn't been tapped. By walking hand in hand with God, right up to the problem, they can reach the fourth dimension of life. God loves them and wants to work with them to create something new in their lives.

Using the four dimensions—length, breadth, depth, and height—He will bring about good in their lives, even in the most seemingly hopeless situations.

1. Length. In response to the question "How long do you want to live?" I replied, "As long as I can." One dimension of life is length, and most people want to live in that dimension.

Many years ago a minister, driving in his buggy along a lonely country road, overtook a young man walking along that road. He stopped and invited him to ride. As they were riding along the minister thought to himself that he had not said anything to this young man about his soul; so in a deep, ministerial voice he said, "Young man, are you prepared to die?"

As the young man went over the back wheel of the buggy, he shouted back, "Not if I can help it."

We read in the Bible, "And all the days of Methuselah were nine hundred sixty and nine years: and he died" (Genesis 5:27). This is the longest life recorded in all history and the shortest biography. The Bible says nothing bad about Methuselah, but neither does it say anything good. Here was a man who just lived. As far as we know he never did any harm, but neither do we know of any good that he did. Methuselah is a monument to how a person might live. However merely living a long time is certainly not the highest goal in life. Other dimensions of life are far more important.

2. Breadth.   We need the dimension of *breadth.* A broad person understands and sympathizes with the people on this earth. There are many differences between people. However three things remain the same the world over: a smile, a tear, and a drop of blood. Those three things represent the most important emotions of mankind. When we come to know each other and understand each other, then we find ourselves concerned with each other.

A man walked through the mist and saw a monster. He raised his gun to fire, but the monster got closer, and he realized it was not a monster, but a man. Again he raised his gun to fire, feeling it would be an enemy who would destroy him. But the man came closer, and he realized it was not only a man, it was his own brother.

We walk through the mists of ignorance, and as we look at each other from a distance we see monsters and enemies, but when we get closer we see brothers. This reflects the two great social doctrines of the fatherhood of God and the brotherhood of man.

Living in the dimension of breadth, one is concerned about

other people. Our Lord told a supreme story about a man who went down from Jerusalem to Jericho. Thieves along the way attacked him, wounded him, robbed him, and left him half dead by the side of the road.

After a while two other men came by and saw the man, but they passed by on the other side and left him there.

Finally a certain Samaritan came by, saw him, had compassion on him, bound up his wounds, put him on his donkey, and took him to an inn where he could be cared for.

Luke 10:30–37 records that story, which represents the three philosophies of life:

First, what belongs to my neighbor belongs to me, and I will take it.

Second, what belongs to me is mine, and I will keep it.

Third, what belongs to me belongs to my brother, and I will share it.

Someone has expressed three philosophies of life in these words: Beat 'em up, pass 'em up, pick 'em up.

In the very first book of the Bible, the question is asked, ". . . Am I my brother's keeper?" (Genesis 4:9). The answer is, "Emphatically, yes." We cannot live just for the sake of living. We are part of the fellowship of mankind on this earth, and that is the second dimension of life.

3. Depth. The third dimension of life is *depth*. If you plan to build a tall building, first, you dig down to form a strong foundation. Jesus told a story of two people who built houses. One built his house upon a rock, and the other built his house upon the sand. When the floods came, the house upon the rocks stood, while the house upon the sand washed away (Matthew 7:24–27). Every life must be built on foundations. That is the dimen-

sion of depth. Faith is one of our foundations. Unless one has
certain convictions about life, sooner or later that person topples
and falls. Friends, reputation, education, skills, all of these form
foundations for living.

On the other hand, if the only thing we had was a foundation, a
building would never rise up into the sky. The foundation makes
possible the heights, which leads us to our fourth dimension.

4. Height.   In *height* we find our dreams, our hopes, our goals,
our ambitions, our ideals. The phrase, "Hitch your wagon to a
star" is good advice. No person can live higher than his dreams.

Once someone asked a mountain climber how he maintained
his strength in climbing the mountain, and his reply was, "I keep
looking up."

The words on the following pages are really about looking up
and reaching the highest peaks of our own lives—our hopes,
goals, dreams, and desires. *This is the fourth dimension of life.*

The Most Precious Tasks of Life

Many people feel disappointed in life. They believe they have
been cheated; they feel God did not give them the abilities, the
resources, the opportunities He gave to someone else. Frequently
I have read the story of the children of Israel building a tabernacle unto God as they moved through the wilderness toward the
Promised Land. You will find this story recorded in the seventh
chapter of the Book of Numbers.

The twelve princes of Israel watched the tabernacle being built.
They did not pretend to understand all the symbolism of the
building, but they were very practical men. They realized this
tabernacle would be very difficult to transport as they marched
through the wilderness. So on the day of dedication, as the people
brought their gifts, these twelve princes did not bring precious

stones or gold; instead they brought six wagons and twelve oxen, which were to be used in transporting the tabernacle.

The responsibility of transporting the tabernacle was in the hands of the sons of three brothers: Gershon, Merari, and Kohath. Moses graciously accepted the wagons and oxen and divided them among those who would be using them. To the sons of Gershon he gave two wagons and four oxen. To the sons of Merari he gave four wagons and eight oxen. Then, we read, "But unto the sons of Kohath he gave none."

Surely the sons of Kohath felt cheated, and it seemed that Moses was unfair. They are not the last ones to feel cheated in life. It seems God gives some people so much more than He gives others.

But before we judge Moses, let us remember how he divided up the work. To the sons of Gershon he gave the responsibility for transporting the top and the sides and the doors of the tabernacle. To the sons of Merari he gave the responsibility for transporting the floors and pillars and the heavy furniture.

However there were some things in the tabernacle too precious to put in a wagon. Some things were too sacred to be pulled by oxen. The altar and the holy things to set upon the altar needed to be carried by hand, and unto the sons of Kohath he gave the responsibility for transporting the precious things of the tabernacle.

So it is in life; the most precious things are done by hand. We have marvelous washing machines for clothes and for dishes, but they have never made a machine to bathe a baby. Babies are bathed by hand.

Someone wrote these words:

> I almost weep when looking back
> To childhood's distant day.
> I think how those hands rested not
> When mine were at their play.

I've looked on hands whose form and hue
A sculptor's dream might be.
Yet are these aged, wrinkled hands,
More beautiful to me.

The author was writing about the hands of his own dear mother, and we can certainly understand those words.

When we feel that we do not have the opportunities somebody else has, let us remember that we have two hands and that we have the opportunity to do the most precious and the most important things in the world.

TWO

Facing Disappointments

One of the bitterest disappointments in all my life came when I was in the third grade. We had a beautifully decorated Christmas tree standing in the corner of the schoolroom. We drew names, and each was supposed to bring a present for the one whose name he or she had drawn. On the morning of the last day of school before Christmas, each one of us came with a brightly wrapped present, and we placed it under the tree. All during that day I kept watching that tree and wondering which present might be mine. Finally the time came to give out the presents. We were all so excited. We sang some Christmas hymns, and the teacher told us the Christmas story. Then she started picking up the presents one by one, calling the name and handing it out to that pupil. Each time I sat there, thinking that the next name called would be mine. Finally only one present sat under the tree, but on that present was the name of a little boy who had not come that day. My name did not appear on any present because that little boy had drawn my name, and not being there, of course he had not brought my present. One of the hard experiences in life is to see life's goodnesses being passed out and your name not being called.

Turning Disappointments Into His Appointments

Many people have found great inspiration in these words of the Psalmist: "Take delight in the Lord, and he will give you the desires of your heart. Commit your way to the Lord; trust in him, and he will act" (Psalms 37:4, 5 RSV). There is glorious peace and power in putting your trust in God and believing that somehow, no matter what happens, things are going to work out for the best. Many times we need to repeat to ourselves the words, "I have changed the world's disappointment into His appointment."

"I Can Start Over in the Morning"

Thomas Carlyle, one of the greatest writers of all time, told about an experience that could have destroyed his entire career. He set out to write a very serious book. It took him four years of hard labor, as, page by page, he wrote that book with his own hand. Finally he completed the last page. Joyously he took the finished manuscript to his friend John Stuart Mill and asked him to read it. It took Mr. Mill several days to read that wonderful manuscript. As he read it he realized that it was truly a great literary achievement. Late one night as he finished the last page he laid the manuscript aside by his chair in the den of his home. The next morning the maid came; seeing those papers on the floor, she thought that they were simply discarded. She threw them into the fire, and they were burned.

When Mr. Mill realized what had happened, he felt deep agony of mind. He went across the field to his friend Carlyle's home and told him that his work of long years had been destroyed.

Carlyle replied, "It's all right. I am sure I can start over in the morning and do it again."

Finally, after great apologies, John Mill left and started back to his home. Carlyle watched his friend walking through the fields and said to his wife, "Poor Mill. I feel so sorry for him. I did not want him to see how crushed I really am."

Then heaving a sigh, he said, "Well, the manuscript is gone, so I had better start writing again."

It was a long, hard process, but he finally completed the work. Thomas Carlyle walked away from his disappointment. He could do nothing about a manuscript that was burned up.

So it is with us: There are times to get up and get going and let what happened happen.

"Take delight in the Lord . . . ," that is, do not get sour or bitter. Keep a smile on your face. No matter what happens, you are going to keep going, keep trusting, keep believing, keep loving, and remember the words ". . . And he will act."

Floods Enrich the Land

Not long ago, I spent the night in a hotel overlooking the Mississippi River. Through the years, I have loved that river, and it never ceases to be an inspiration to me. I sat in my room, and I looked out over the river, thinking about the song:

> He don't plant 'taters, he don't plant cotton,
> Them that plants it are soon forgotten,
> But Old Man River just keeps on rollin' along.

As I sat looking at the river I began to remember that there were times when the old Mississippi was not always so peaceful and tranquil. Sometimes the river overflowed its banks—the crops were ruined, houses were destroyed, people were hurt by it.

However, through the long years each flood has left a deposit of rich topsoil. Gradually the floods have enriched the land, and some of the most fertile land in all the nation includes the delta area of the Mississippi.

The floods of disappointment, frustration, sorrow, and all the others come sweeping over our lives. But we keep on going, and somehow out of the disappointments we find ourselves enriched. After the flood, the beauty of life becomes even more beautiful.

A person can be wounded. Life sometimes cuts deeply and hurts terribly. If we do not cleanse them carefully, our wounds can become infected. Bitterness is an infection—so is anger or hatred or jealousy or worry. The wounds of life can foster discouragement and hopelessness—a "what's the use?" spirit. Hurt lives can be wrecked and destroyed. On the other hand, no matter what happens, we need to keep believing the words of the Psalmist: "Delight thyself also in the Lord; and he shall give thee the desires of thine heart" (Psalms 37:4). Let the floods come, but we keep a right spirit, and out of the wounds of life will come our greatest blessings.

"Acquaint Thyself With Him and Be at Peace"

Every year we see marvelous and wonderful progress in the field of medical science. At one time diphtheria was one of the dreaded diseases of mankind. But today, nobody is afraid of diphtheria; it has practically been eliminated. So has smallpox, and thank God, so has polio. Pneumonia used to be a dreaded disease, but today, the physicians have medicines that can deal with pneumonia. Great progress has been made in the field of cancer.

Medical science marches on to new heights.

However, in spite of all the great progress in medicine, our doctors' offices are more crowded today than ever before.

Perhaps much of the illness of today is in the person's mind. Maybe we do not make too much progress in the areas of worry, fear, stress, overwork and underrest, alcohol, diet, anxiety and tension, and such things. We thank God for the medicines that protect our bodies from the enemies that would destroy. We also need more than medicine for the protection of our minds.

Instead of looking for something new, we might go back to one of the oldest books that we have—the Book of Job in the Bible. Job had a lot of problems: He lost his wealth, all his children were killed, he lost his health and was deserted by his friends. Finally even his wife turned away from him, but Job never lost the faith. And perhaps the answer is found in Job 22:21: "Acquaint now thyself with him, and be at peace. . . ." Marvelous power exists in that admonition of Job's. He would say the same thing to our worried, fast-moving society today.

Most of us are better acquainted with our troubles than with God. However as I read this suggestion in Job 22 I find listed there seven marvelous results for one who does what Job told them to do, "Acquaint now thyself with him. . . ."

1. "Good shall come unto thee" (verse 21). That does not mean that everything that happens will be good. It *does* mean that when we become acquainted with God, there comes into our lives a special quality and strength that somehow ultimately brings good to us.

2. "Thou shalt be built up" (verse 23). Here God promises both physical healing, because Job was a sick man in body, and lifted spirits: a new strength, power, vitality.

3. "Then shalt thou lay up gold" (verse 24). It is so easy to become worried about finances. We live in a world where material needs are very real. God created all wealth there is, and He still controls it, so what do we have to worry about?

4. "Then shalt thou have thy delight in the Almighty" (verse 26). When one says, "I am delighted," it means joy and satisfaction; it means peace and happiness. What a wonderful state in which to live!

5. "Thou shalt also decree a thing, and it shall be established unto thee" (verse 28). That is, you will not be defeated and frustrated any longer. You will know what it means to succeed at something you want to accomplish.

6. "Light shall shine upon thy ways" (verse 28). Instead of stumbling along in darkness and groping in the haze of fear, you will see a way in which you can walk.

7. "When men are cast down, then thou shalt say, There is lifting up" (verse 29). Though life has a way of knocking us down, it cannot keep us down.

How are these seven things accomplished? Let us read again, "Acquaint now thyself with him." As we saturate our minds with the power, the goodness, the love of God, these seven things will happen to us. The twenty-second chapter of the Book of Job is truly an inspiration.

Too Busy? Pray

Early in life I was taught to pray, and I have never ceased. Every day, several times, I pray. I pray when I am so busy I do not have time to pray. I know that when I do not have time to pray, then it is time to pray. We will find a marvelous relief from tension and anxiety as we yield ourselves to God's will. After I pray, then I go back to my job, and I realize that I can get more work done than I accomplished before. My mind is clearer; I have a greater sense of power and joy and satisfaction. I feel more creative.

Commitment Brings Courage

The Prophet Isaiah said, "And thine ears shall hear a word behind thee, saying, This is the way, walk ye in it ..." (Isaiah

30:21). We are not compelled to walk alone through life. Neither must we remain dependent upon our own wisdom. We may abide in the supporting presence of the eternal God and His guidance.

The first and greatest decision toward making life worthwhile is commitment to God's way and God's will. If you say, "I have never heard the voice of God behind me," you may need to remember that God does not waste His breath. He speaks only to people who are ready and willing to listen. Hearing the voice of God, you need to begin walking.

A young bear cub was puzzled about how to walk. The little bear asked the mother bear, "Shall I move my right foot first or my left, or the two front feet together and then my back feet, or my feet on one side together and then the ones on the other side?" The mother bear simply said, "Leave off thinking and just begin walking."

You concentrate on your problems, and you get confused. Make up your mind you are going to walk God's way, no matter what happens. You make one decision, and the other decisions of life just fall into place. You begin getting somewhere.

In the second place, a consciousness that you are walking in God's way enables you to face the future with anticipation, instead of apprehension. Most of the confusion and disturbance in our minds result from fear of what might happen in the future. Someone has said that 40 percent of our fears are things that might happen in the future; 12 percent are of some imaginary illness; 10 percent are fears for loved ones; 30 percent are over something that happened in the past, about which nothing that can now be done. Only 8 percent of our fears have real causes.

The way to rid your mind of fear is through the substitution of stronger thoughts. When you feel the voice of God in your heart, fears disappear, and you move triumphantly through life. Years ago, I read a story that Ernest Holmes told. He was in a hotel room in San Francisco, his phone rang, and a voice said, "I am in six-oh-six, and I am in trouble." Mr. Holmes discovered the man was drinking, but he was quite rational. He went to see him. On the table was a bottle half filled with whiskey. He listened to the man's story, in which he said that he lacked the power to break the hold that alcohol had upon him.

Ernest Holmes said, "You stay here. I am going to my room to pray. I will leave the bottle beside you, but you will never finish it." In his room Holmes began to picture in his mind that man having the power to resist his craving. He thought about the strength he could possess by the grace of God. He formed his prayer to fit the picture of this man. As he prayed he concentrated upon the man's strength instead of his weakness. Holmes reported that early the next morning his phone rang. "Come here quickly," the man said. When Holmes got there, he saw that none of the liquor was gone from the bottle. The man was pacing the floor. He said, "Last night I felt that God was in this room. I conquered my desire. I am now set free."

There are two comments upon that story that I wish to make: When one takes God into his life he begins to concentrate on his powers, instead of problems; when one finds fellowship with God, he has strengths that overcome every weakness. You cannot be the same person after you become God's person. Commitment of life gives a courageous heart.

Sustained and Strengthened

In his play *Candle in the Wind,* Maxwell Anderson tells the story of a young American girl pitted against the ruthless Nazi rulers of occupied Paris. She was only a young girl, as he put it, just a "candle in the wind." But the feeling that she was an American citizen sustained and strengthened her. She felt that behind her was the might and power of her beloved nation and that her cause was one of justice and right.

Sometimes we feel no stronger than a "candle in the wind." But when we experience the assurance of God's power and presence, we become sustained and strengthened.

Whittier said it beautifully in *The Eternal Goodness:*

> Yet, in the maddening maze of things,
> And tossed by storm and flood,
> To one fixed trust my spirit clings;
> I know that God is good.

Strength That Makes Living Fun

Henry van Dyke wrote these marvelous words:

This is the gospel of labour, ring it, ye bells of the kirk!
The Lord of Love came down from above, to live with men who work.

Many people feel overburdened; their day's work seems just too much. However many people have learned that there are resources available equal to the very hardest work and biggest job. The Bible gives us a marvelous promise: "But they that wait upon the Lord shall renew their strength; they shall mount up with wings as eagles; they shall run, and not be weary; and they shall walk, and not faint" (Isaiah 40:31).

Someone asked Thomas Edison why he worked so hard. He replied, "I have not worked a day in my life; I have just had a good time."

We can rise above those things that hurt—the disappointments, defeat, and wearisome hours—and we can find the strength that makes living so much fun.

The Rhythm of the Universe in Each of Us

Dr. Norman Vincent Peale has been one of the greatest in-spirations in my life. I have never heard him speak or read any-thing he wrote that was not a blessing to me. In fact, no minister has inspired America the way Dr. Peale has. I remember hearing him tell about a lady who finally just broke down under the strain of living: the daily pressures, her worries and fears, her hurts and disappointments. She went to the beach to spend a few days, just to quietly rest. One day, sitting out on the beach, her body was in such a position that she became conscious of the beating of her own pulse. She noticed there was a definite rhythm in her pulse, which fascinated her.

As she felt the rhythm within her own body, she happened to notice the tall beach grass all around her, which had been washed clean by the tide. A gentle breeze blew the grass back and forth, back and forth, back and forth. To her astonishment, she realized that the moving of the sea breeze also had a rhythm—a rhythm very much akin to the rhythm within her own body.

She lifted her eyes and began to watch the rise and fall of the sea. She saw the waves slowly coming in across white sand. To her astonishment, she realized the rise and fall of the water of the mighty ocean also followed a rhythm. It was the same rhythm that the grass had and that she had felt within herself.

Suddenly she caught the point: A human being, the beach grass, the mighty ocean are all part of one creation, and over them all is the mighty God. As she lay on the beach, she realized that the power within the universe also worked within her. She felt her strength renewed, that she could even "run, and not be weary."

When we find ourselves attuned to the rhythm of God, we find renewed strength.

"Let the Peace of God Rule in Your Hearts"

Oftentimes when I feel tired or tense or worried or frightened, I get great comfort out of quoting to myself, six or eight times, the words of Saint Paul, "And let the peace of God rule in your hearts . . ." (Colossians 3:15). To say those words over and over makes me feel good and relaxed. Too many times our hearts are ruled by turmoil instead of peace.

Enrico Caruso, the great singer, would hold a very fragile glass between his thumb and forefinger. He would sing an ascending scale, holding a high note, and suddenly the glass would shatter into pieces under the vibration.

That same thing can happen to people. High-frequency nervous tension can wreak havoc on human personalities and bodies. There is no way of escaping the vicissitudes of human existence. But when the peace of God rules within our hearts, we feel confident and supreme. It was William Cullen Bryant who wrote:

> He who, from zone to zone,
> Guides through the boundless sky thy certain flight,
> In the long way that I must tread alone,
> Will lead my steps aright.

Robert Louis Stevenson said it this way: "Quiet minds cannot be perplexed or frightened but go on in fortune or in misfortune at their own private pace like the ticking of a clock during a thunderstorm." That is a beautiful analogy. No matter how hard the wind blows or how loud the thunder crashes, the clock does not change its pace. It keeps its same steady ticktock, ticktock, ticktock.

I get a new thrill every time I read Captain Eddie Rickenbacker's story of three awful weeks on a little raft lost in the far Pacific. When asked how they were able to endure that experi-

ence, his simple, unaffected explanation was: "We prayed." For
days they had drifted helplessly under the scorching tropic sun.
Their feet became blistered, their faces burned, their mouths and
bodies parched. The heat, the hunger, the exhaustion, brought
them to the breaking point. The men with him were young and
inexperienced, facing their first great trial. But Eddie Rickenbacker believed in prayer. He had learned to pray at his mother's
knee, and in all the crises of his life, prayer had given him the
comfort and courage he needed. On the eighth day of hunger and
thirst and fear, some of the men were alarmingly desperate. That
day they read these words from the New Testament: "Take no
thought for your life, what ye shall eat, or what ye shall drink; nor
yet for your body, what ye shall put on. . . . But seek ye first the
kingdom of God, and his righteousness; and all these things shall
be added unto you" (Matthew 6:25, 33). And they prayed.

What happened next seemed like a miracle, and who can say it
was not? A sea gull flew in out of nowhere and landed on Rickenbacker's head. They had food. Also they had bait for two fish-
hooks they had. Then came their first rainstorm, and they had
water. From then on they prayed with renewed confidence. They
calmed down because they believed God was with them.

They continued to drift for nearly two weeks, but they continued to believe. On the twenty-first day they were spotted by a
plane. It was truly a miraculous rescue, for the rafts were tiny little dots on the vast surface of the ocean. To be seen, a plane had
to fly almost directly above them. And in answer to everybody,
Rickenbacker simply said, "We prayed."

Affirm to yourself, "The peace of God is ruling in my heart."
Say it again and again until it becomes fixed in your thinking.
Then go on with your activities, but pause frequently to say, "The
peace of God is ruling in my heart." Keep it up day by day, and
you will see that God's ruling will bring you quiet calmness and
power.

Grow a Soul

We have always been concerned about the growth and development of our physical bodies, but many times we neglect to realize that we each have a spiritual self and that, if we are to experience the high joys of life, we must nourish and develop our spiritual selves. As someone put it, "Every person must grow a soul."

Three men go to a great concert. The first one is a musician to his fingertips. He knows and understands and loves the music. He traces with delight every repetition of the theme through all the variations of an intricate fugue.

The second man has not the musical soul of the first man, but he enjoys it as much as he can. His limited capacity limits his enjoyment of the music.

The third man is bored completely. He secretly longs for the end. To him it is punishment to sit there.

In some degree that is the way people experience the business of living. We fail to "grow our souls" because we do not use our spiritual capacities; they lie dormant within us. The fish in Mammoth Cave have eyes, but they cannot see. They have lived in darkness through generations, and not being used, their eyes become sightless. So it is with any of our faculties: Quit praying, and one gets to the point where prayer becomes very difficult indeed.

In our spiritual growth, we may easily develop a false optimism that prevents immediate effort. Some day we plan to consider our spiritual natures, but we are too busy now with other things.

More tragically some people remain satisfied with the state they are in. They dream no more dreams; they feel no more call of the Spirit of God; they are not stirred by the impulses of their hearts.

The great sculptor Bertel Thorvaldsen noticed the waning of

his power when he stood before a statue he had just completed and he felt satisfied. The tragedy was that his hand had caught up with his dreams.

On the other hand, the great Saint Paul said: "Brethren, I count not myself to have apprehended. . . . I press toward the mark . . ." (Philippians 3:13, 14). He said those words near the end of a long and triumphant life, but he realized there was still a ways to go. Self-satisfaction is a deadly state of mind.

S. H. Hadley was born in Ohio in the year 1842. He studied medicine and had all the promise of being a great physician, but he began drinking and became addicted to it. He eventually found himself in New York City, and there he reached the place where he was homeless, friendless, and financially destitute. He thought about committing suicide. Then he wrote these words:

> Toward the evening one day the idea came to my head to go to Jerry MaCauley's mission. There I heard MaCauley tell of his deliverance from drinking, and there I listened to the testimony of a number of others, all of them saved from a fate like mine. I made up my mind I would be saved too, or die right there. When the invitation was given I went forward and knelt. What a conflict was going on in my soul. Something within me said, Come. Something else said, Be careful. I hesitated for a moment, and then with a breaking heart I cried, Dear Jesus can you save me? Never can I describe what had happened. I only know I was suddenly a free man again.

It is a fact of life that when one becomes dissatisfied, feels the need for something beyond one's own strength, somehow there is a power which literally reaches to us and picks us up. Whatever our weakness, there is a strength available to us which is more than enough to overcome that weakness.

In his book entitled *South,* Sir Ernest Shackleton tells of an experience in which he and his men were marooned far in the Antarctic. They were forced to make a long, perilous trip over unnamed mountain glaciers. One slip and they would have been lost. He writes:

> When I look back at those days I have no doubt that Providence guided us across the storm-swept sea, which separated Elephant Island from civilization. I know that during that march over the mountains and glaciers it often seemed to me that we were four and not three. I said nothing to my companions at this point, but after Worsley said to me, "I had a curious feeling on the march that there was another person with us." Crean, the third member of our little group, then confessed to the same feeling. One realizes the dearth of human words, the roughness of mortal speech in trying to describe things intangible, but a record of our journey would be incomplete without at least a reference to a subject very near to our hearts.

Sometimes people say that they have never had this feeling of divine presence. Once a lady stood watching J. M. W. Turner, a great artist, as he painted a glorious sunset. She commented, "But Mr. Turner, I never see any sunsets like yours."

"But madam," he replied, "Don't you wish you could?"

When we hear of people feeling God's presence, there is a longing in our hearts for that same experience. At times it would be worth more than anything on this earth, and I can say to every one of us that it is possible as we give spiritual things their proper place in our lives.

THREE
Overcoming Failures

The Book of Ecclesiastes is really a dreary book. If we feel miserable and sour, downhearted and pessimistic, and are looking for something to read to fit those moods, then Ecclesiastes will suit us. It was written by a man who lost hope and heart. To him life had been drained of all of its sweetness, and there was nothing left to look forward to. The rising sun on a new day brought to him no thrill of expectancy, so he cried out, ". . . Vanity of vanities; all is vanity" (Ecclesiastes 1:2). He had become cynical. My dictionary says that *cynical* means to be "sneering" or "sarcastic"; it is to have, the dictionary points out, "contempt for or disbelief in the virtues of others."

The writer of Ecclesiastes saw five things in life that he had given up on and saw no good in them:

1. In the physical universe, he pointed out, the sun goes up and goes down, the wind whirls about continually, and all the rivers run to the sea, and yet the sea is never full. To him the physical world was just a hopeless failure. He could never have understood the words of Elizabeth Barrett Browning, who looked out and found the earth literally "crammed with heaven, And every common bush afire with God." The Psalmist looked into the heavens and heard them declaring the glory of God, but this

man looked out on God's world and said, "Life here is just a wretched, monotonous treadmill."

2. Pleasure he also found hopeless. He exclaimed, "I said in mine heart, Go to now, I will prove thee with mirth, therefore enjoy pleasure: and, behold, this also is vanity" (Ecclesiastes 2:1). To him all the joy of life was gone; there was no reason to laugh; there was nothing to make him happy.

3. Achievements were also vanity. He wanted to accomplish something. He set out to do great things. He built houses, planted vineyards, built lakes, accumulated wealth, had servants, and became powerful. Yet after he had done all these things, he threw up his hands in disgust and declared it all vanity, because you die and leave it all, and it's somebody else's. In other words, "You can't take it with you," therefore it is not worth the effort to get it.

4. Of wisdom he said, "And I turned myself to behold wisdom. . . ." But he came to the conclusion it is probably better to be a happy fool than a wretched wise man. He would have agreed with the statement "Where ignorance is bliss, 'tis folly to be wise." Even though he became wise, he declared, ". . . And how dieth the wise man? as the fool" (2:16).

5. He even gave up on humanity itself. He decided that all people are bad, or at least nearly all people. He counted people one by one and came to the conclusion that maybe one man out of a thousand is worthy, but he did not find even one worthy woman. "Which yet my soul seeketh, but I find not: one man among a thousand have I found; but a woman among all those have I not found" (Ecclesiastes 7:28).

He despaired of the world ever getting any better. He reasoned, "Consider the work of God: for who can make that straight, which he hath made crooked?" (Ecclesiastes 7:13). His loss of faith in life and in God's world and purposes killed his sense of obligation, made him unhappy and most miserable.

Sometimes, as an antidote for depression, the Book of Ecclesiastes works. As one reads it carefully one sees wisdom and understanding in it. Out of his despair the writer came to realize the importance of God and God's way. Triumphantly he said, "Let us hear the conclusion of the whole matter: Fear God, and keep his commandments: for this is the whole duty of man" (Ecclesiastes 12:13).

He realized that he missed life because he left God out.

When We Run Out of Gas

"But they that wait upon the Lord shall renew their strength; they shall mount up with wings as eagles; they shall run, and not be weary; and they shall walk, and not faint" (Isaiah 40:31).

The mere reading of those words is as refreshing as the sound of a running stream on a hot summer day. Those words sound as melodious as the tones of a great pipe organ in a beautiful cathedral. More important, they give us the secret to how to keep going.

The other day my car suddenly stopped. I looked at the gauge on the dashboard and saw that I was out of gasoline. I might have called a mechanic and had him come and replace every worn part of the car, but still it would not have run. I might have had a new set of the finest tires put on it, but still it would have sat there. I might have washed and polished my car until it was as bright and shining as new; still it would have gone no place.

My car had exhausted its power, and until a new supply of gasoline was put in the tank, the car would be dead and lifeless. When God made this universe, He provided marvelous power for mankind to use—oil and gas in the ground, electricity in the air, atomic power all about us. Man's progress has been determined by his ability to harness and use that power. If the sources of our power were suddenly cut off, all progress would come to a screeching halt.

Many times we "do not feel good" or "are all run down" or "do not have any energy." People, like automobiles, can run out of gas. We can take vitamins and tonics, go on vacations, play golf, go fishing, look at television, read novels, and on and on, but the prophet in the long ago was right when he said, "But they that wait upon the Lord shall renew their strength." There comes a time when only God in our lives gives us the power we need to keep going.

I personally think that going to church is a very important function in the lives of people. I am not against having church services on television. I have been preaching on television probably longer than any other preacher in the entire world. Almost every Sunday since 1949 I have spoken on television, but television is not like being present in the church. When I first started out as a preacher, I decided it would be a good thing to go to the church during the week and practice my sermon as I stood in the pulpit. But I soon gave that up. The reason was that without the people in the pews the sermon in the pulpit was meaningless. The important thing was not the sermon, but the response of people; and when those people are gathered together, it becomes a more meaningful and powerful experience.

It has been well said:

> We mutter and sputter,
> We fume and we spurt,
> We mumble and groan,
> Our feelings are hurt;
> We can't understand things,
> Our vision grows dim,
> But all that we need,
> Is a moment with Him.
>
> AUTHOR UNKNOWN

As we "wait upon the Lord" sometimes we have an instantaneous flow of power. Sometimes there comes an immediate answer to some problem that has worried us for years. On the other hand, more often that new life and strength come to us through the process of cultivation and growth. However it comes, maintaining the conscious contact with God always gets the person going again.

"I Almost Fainted"

In the Twenty-seventh Psalm, David tells us how he almost fainted. That is, that he almost gave up on life. Sooner or later every one of us experiences this. We are going our way, and somehow we begin to wonder if it is worth the effort. Some people do quit and bow out of life. All of us can say as the Psalmist said, "I almost fainted." However, he did not faint, and in the Twenty-seventh Psalm, he did tell how he kept from quitting and how he kept on going. Every so often, I feel that the Twenty-seventh Psalm is the one I really need.

As I read this Psalm, I find myself underscoring such words as:

The Lord is my light and my salvation; whom shall I fear?

In the time of trouble he shall hide me.

Hear, O Lord, when I cry with my voice: have mercy also upon me, and answer me.

Thou hast been my help; leave me not.

When my father and my mother forsake me, then the Lord will take me up.

I had fainted, unless I had believed to see the goodness of the Lord in the land of the living.

Wait on the Lord: be of good courage, and he shall strengthen thine heart.

In the first place, when you put your faith in God, it gives you faith in yourself. One of the greatest obstacles in the pathway to a worthwhile life is the feeling of insecurity. We all feel inadequate and overcome by the sense of inferiority. Feeling inadequate, we have a tendency to pretend superiority, then begin to bluff and bully our way through life.

On the other hand, feeling inadequate, we can retreat into a world of daydreams. Unable to face real life, we can create illusions of how we would like it to be.

The Psalmist almost fainted when he looked out into a world and saw, as he put it, ". . . False witnesses are risen up against me. . . ." Time and again we reach a place when we wonder if all the world is against us. In the fourth century, there lived a great theologian named Athanasius. So strongly did he stand for certain principles that were unpopular that there arose a saying, "Athanasius against the world." Had you looked behind the scenes, however, you would have found that Athanasius had friends and supporters who kept him going.

Some time ago, in another city, I became acquainted with a man who lost both legs in an accident. People marveled at his courage and his high spirit. He told me that he almost gave up and quit, but he had a wife who loved him; whenever he was despondent and blue, she kept saying over and over to him, "Do not worry, I will always stay with you. I have two legs, and I can do the walking for you." It was her spirit that kept him going.

The Psalmist not only had some friends, but when he believed in God, he believed in the future: ". . . unless I had believed to see the goodness of the Lord in the land of the living." He believed that God would not only accomplish His will in the hereafter, but also in the here and now. The most paralyzing disaster in human nature is a persistent fear of tomorrow.

A boy born with a deformed leg had to wear a brace from the time he first began to walk. As he grew older he found he could not compete with other boys in sports. He could not run or even climb trees. Gradually he built up a feeling of inferiority. Because he felt inadequate, he developed an intense fear of life. If he could not climb a tree, how could he ever climb the ladder of life?

The brace was not only on his leg; it had gotten into his mind.

His father told him not to worry. Someday he would take the boy to the great cathedral, and there God would heal his leg. Finally the day came when they were to go to the cathedral. He dressed in his best clothes. When they got to the cathedral and walked down the aisle, he could hear the brace on his leg thumping every step. He wondered if anybody around heard that thumping noise. Finally the time came for them to kneel at the altar. The father said, "Son, pray and ask God to heal you." Finally the father said, "Amen." He put his arm about the boy and said, "Son, let us give thanks to God. You are healed."

The boy said that he had never seen such a look on his father's face as he saw that day. It was a look of relief, triumph, and joy. They started down the aisle, the brace on his leg thumping just as before, but suddenly the boy said he felt the wondrously warm glow in his heart. All of a sudden he was happy. Later he explained what happened. God had not taken the brace off his leg, but He had taken the brace out of his mind. The remainder of his life he carried that brace on his leg, but he had so yielded to the marvelous power of faith that he never again feared it.

Four Lessons for Life

One of the most fascinating Bible stories is the one about two mothers claiming the same baby. They lived together in the same house, and both had given birth to babies about the same time. One baby died. The mothers came to King Solomon. One said that the other woman's child had died in the night, and that woman arose and took her living son from her side and laid the dead child next to her. When she woke up and saw the dead child, after carefully looking at the child, she realized it was not the one she had given birth to. However, the other woman said, "No that did not happen; it was her child who died and not mine." So they asked King Solomon to settle the dispute as to who was the rightful mother of the living child.

Solomon, being a very wise man, immediately saw the way to settle the issue. He said, "Bring me a sword." The king said, "Divide the living child in two, and give half to the one and half to the other."

One of the women agreed to that settlement, but the other mother began to cry and said, "Oh, my lord, give her the living child, and in no wise slay it." The king decided that she was, in truth, the mother of the child, so he awarded the child to her. He realized that the one who would rather give up the child than see it killed was the real mother. You can read this story in 1 Kings 3:16–28. It is not only a story with great human interest, but also one that teaches us some of the most important lessons in life.

1. The Futility of the Sword.   The first lesson we see here is the futility of the sword. Suppose Solomon had actually used the sword and cut the baby in half? Neither of the mothers would have had a live baby, and the world would have been forever robbed of a life.

After the First World War, Sherwood Eddy, a very wise man, summed up that war in these words: "The saddest thing is not that some ten million of our best men are dead, that the world is impoverished, victimized, embittered by hate, rent by suspicion and fear. It is that we have settled nothing, made nothing safe, achieved no lasting good." The fact that he was right, everlastingly right, is proven by the fact that the next generation did it all over again in what we called the Second World War. When the Second World War was all over, all the issues that started the war remained. Nothing was settled.

We need to learn life's lesson that we do not settle anything by fighting. Not by fighting with our wives or husbands, not by fighting with our parents or children, not by fighting with the people we work with, not by fighting with anybody. You do not win by fighting your way through life.

2. The Limits of Compromise. In that story of the living baby, King Solomon demonstrated the limits of compromise. Many times compromise makes trading possible. If one person wants to buy something from another person, it may be that the buyer will not be willing to give the asking price, so he will offer a lower price. Then the seller will say, "No, but I will come down from my asking price," so they go until they reach a price on which they can both agree.

In this connection I have a silly story. A boy proposed to a girl. She accepted his proposal on the condition that he would save $1,000. He got a job in another city and went off to seek his fortune. She did not hear from him for nearly a year; in fact, she was getting a bit worried. Finally he came back. She asked him, "Have you saved the thousand dollars?" "No," he replied, "I have saved only thirty-five dollars so far." "Well," she answered, "that's near enough. Let's get married."

We like people who are willing to compromise, who do not insist on having their own way all the time. There are occasions when we need to give in to each other. Compromise plays a very important role in the home and business and through our lives. No person should always completely insist on his or her way.

On the other hand, there are times when compromise is the very wrong thing to attempt. This baby belonged either to one mother or the other. Dividing it between them was not possible.

No compromise can be achieved in mathematics. Two times two is four. It makes no difference what the circumstances are; there is no way that two times two can be anything else but four.

Music does not allow compromise. Harmony is produced by

strict observance of certain laws. The same thing might be said of many scientific principles.

At times no compromise is possible in questions of right and wrong and questions of good and evil. Either God exists or He does not. There is no compromise on that question. Neither can we compromise in the fields of honesty or integrity or in the principles of good and evil. Every person has certain foundation beliefs that cannot be compromised without the person being severely hurt.

3. *The Best Things in Life Cannot Be Divided.* The baby could not be divided. There are two types of things in the world: quantities and entities. A pound of butter is a quantity. If you have a pound of butter, you can give half to a friend and keep the other half. The same can be said of a dozen eggs or a quart of milk. A beggar might come to you, and you can share your bread with him. On the other hand, you cannot share your coat with him. A piece of bread is a quantity, so is a pound of butter or a quart of milk; but a coat is an entity, and it cannot be divided without being destroyed. Your watch cannot be cut in half and be preserved, neither can a beautiful painting, a lovely song, an inspiring poem, or a beautiful rose. Some of the best and most important things in life cannot be divided.

Marriage is an example. If one would have the joy of marriage, one also must assume the responsibility.

The Christian faith is an entity. We like the comfort we get from the words, "Come unto me, all ye that labour and are heavy laden, and I will give you rest" (Matthew 11:28). We like to take the words of comfort, but forget the challenge that says, "Take my yoke upon you, and learn of me . . ." (Matthew 11:29). Today we find many Christian people who forget the challenge but are grateful for the comfort. The Christian faith cannot be divided; it is an entity.

4. *A Realm Beyond Mathematics.* There is a realm in life where mathematics does not apply. We say that two times two is always four. If we find one instance where two times two is five or three, then we would destroy all mathematics.

On the other hand half a baby plus half a baby does not equal a whole baby, and there are many other instances of this. I stood with a young couple recently as we buried their baby who had died. You cannot explain that experience simply by saying that three minus one equals two. The realm of mathematics does not explain many of life's most important experiences.

A father and mother can make their wills and leave their wealth to their children, but they can give to each child only a share of their wealth. However, when that couple's first child was born, they gave to that child all their love. After a while a second child was born, and they gave all their love to that second child; yet they loved the first child just as much. They could have had four children or six children or eight children and given to each of their children all their love. Love is a realm where mathematics does not apply.

FOUR
Moving Ahead With Enthusiasm

Saint Paul had a "thorn in the flesh." We do not know what it was; it may have been one of any number of handicaps. He prayed three times for it to be taken away from him, but God told him "My grace is sufficient for thee . . ." (2 Corinthians 12:9).

Every person has some problem or difficulty that has the power to hurt us in life. Many of us have prayed more than three times that it might be removed, and many times God does change the circumstances. But there are times when He does for us what He did for Saint Paul. He does not take away the problem, but gives us the strength, the intelligence, the ability, the will to deal with it.

If you have a life-insurance policy, you know that there is a so-called grace period, usually lasting thirty days. After your premium comes due, you still have that period of thirty days in which to make your payment. That means that the life-insurance company really carries your policy for you for that length of time. But it is a limited grace.

Not so with the grace of God. To Saint Paul, God said, "My grace is sufficient for thee. . . ." Underscore that word *sufficient*. That means it does not run out. There is no end to it; it is the power to overcome any difficulty, any disability, any weakness.

When we sing our national anthem, "The Star-Spangled Banner," usually we sing the first verse. If you want to hear almost dead silence, ask a group of people to sing the second verse of our great national hymn. "The Star-Spangled Banner" was written by Francis Scott Key in the year 1814. During the British attack on Baltimore, a terrible night in which struggling colonies faced the resources of the British Empire, all night long the heavy guns pounded Fort Henry. In the morning, however, the author saw "by the dawn's early light" that the flag was still waving; thus he was inspired to write his famous song, which became our national anthem. The first verse is marvelous and stirring, but sometime it would help us to read all the way through and read the last words of that great song:

> Then conquer we must, when our cause it is just;
> And this be our motto: "In God is our trust!"
> And the star-spangled banner in triumph shall wave
> O'er the land of the free and the home of the brave.

There are times when we need to underscore those words *then conquer we must*. We need to believe that "God's grace is sufficient," if we know that we are on the right path. If our "cause is just," then we can be certain that somehow we are not going to be defeated. Great and wonderful forces stand beside the person who has faith and, no matter what happens, holds to that faith. Saint Paul never did overcome his handicap, but on the other hand, he was never defeated by it either. We need to remember that.

Decide and Get Going

One woman had had a very difficult time. She had been divorced under rather tragic circumstances. She tried working at several different jobs, but none of them turned out well for her. Finally she decided she was sick. Often people find that getting sick is a very convenient method of escape. After seeing several doctors, she discovered none could help her. She visited a psychiatrist, but still she was no better off. Finally she came to see me. I told her she had had all the counseling I was capable of giving her, and I didn't know that I could add anything to what she had already been through. Then I said, "Let me say to you that you can live in the past, brood over what has happened, condemn yourself and others, and be miserably sick the rest of your life. On the other hand, you can start right now and make for yourself a new life."

She decided she wanted to live again, so I told her the first step was to go home, take a sheet of paper, and write down two questions: What would I like to do more than anything else? How can I get started doing that right now? She needed what we all need: a goal and a starting place. When those two things are thoroughly fixed, then we begin to move.

One of many people's favorite Bible chapter is John 14, one of the farewell talks that Jesus had with His disciples. He started off by telling them of His Father's house and that He was about to leave them. Certainly they were worried and even frightened. They had given up all they had to follow Him. They had seen Him work marvelous miracles; they had heard Him speak in such a way that ". . . the common people heard him gladly" (Mark 12:37). So they were shocked when He said to them, ". . . He that believeth on me, the works that I do shall he do also; and greater works than these shall he do . . ." (John 14:12). This was really a mind-boggling statement that they could do even greater things than He had done. But then He added these words, "And whatsoever ye shall ask in my name, that will I do . . ." (John 14:13). That was a firm, unconditional promise.

Dr. Leslie Weatherhead said that once, when he was a high school student, he had a very difficult examination. He had discovered that verse, "And whatsoever ye shall ask in my name, that will I do. . . ." He believed that God would see to it that he passed his examination. He told God he was believing His promise, and he wanted a good grade on the exam. The next day he took the examination, but when the grades were in, he had failed. He rebelled and almost lost his faith. He thought that the promises of the Bible were not good. The next year he repeated that course. He worked hard, and he passed; then he decided that he did not need God, that he could get along by himself.

It took him some years to understand that his own powers and abilities were in reality the power that God had given to him. He also realized that God had already given him the power to pass the examination, but he had not used that power the first go-around. God never gives us more power than we need. Until we are willing to use what God has already given us, there is no need to ask for any more.

So the substance of the matter is, you have the power right now, so decide what you want and get going. Later on, after you have given your very best, if you need more, God will supply it. As of the moment, however, you have enough.

Love Comes Back

The most creative, constructive power on this earth is the power of love. Love is like a boomerang: Send it forth, and it comes back to you with even greater force. There is a poem that tells us: "Give love and love to your heart will flow, a strength in your utmost need."

Elias Howe, a man broken in health and poverty stricken, felt his life was over. Day by day he watched his wife slowly sewing in order to get them a little money for the next meal. Beyond and above all things, Howe loved his wife, and it hurt him to watch her work so hard.

Because of his love for her, he forgot his sick body and began thinking how he might help her. He went to work and, six months later, had completed the first model of his sewing machine. It made him famous and rich, and it also made him well. The power of a great love came back to bless him.

Alexander Graham Bell, a great benefactor of mankind, taught in a school for the deaf. He fell in love and married one of his pupils. She could not hear, and because Bell loved her, he suffered because of her handicap.

The consuming passion of his life was to do something to help the one he loved. He decided it would be possible to develop a hearing aid, and he set to work. He never counted the hours he spent working on it; he only knew he wanted to help one he loved. In the process of his experimentation, he developed the telephone. The love he gave came back to him as a creative, constructive force.

The very moment you fall in love with a great idea or a great cause or a great purpose or another person, you become creative. Life takes on new meaning and a new direction. You forget the failures of the past; you develop new faith and new powers. Pessimism, doubt, despair, discouragements, and all your negative attitudes are expelled under the power of a great love.

Charlotte Perkins Gilman has expressed it in a poem:

> Shall we not open the human heart,
> Swing the doors till the hinges start;
> Stop our worrying, doubt and din,
> Hunting heaven and dodging sin?
> There is no need to search so wide,
> Open the door and stand aside—
> Let God in!

But we cannot stop there. The power of God is like electricity; it will not go in unless it can also come out. God's power is always for a purpose. So the next verse of the poem is:

Shall we not open the human heart,
To loving labor in field and mart;
Working together for all about,
The good, large labor that knows no doubt?
Can He be held in our narrow rim?
Do the work that is work for Him—
Let God out!

". . . God is love" says the Bible (1 John 4:8). Through love you find God. Henry George said, "I loved the people, and that love brought me to Christ as their best friend and teacher." Cardinal Henry E. Manning replied, "And I loved Christ, and so learned to love the people for whom He died."

Enthusiasm Reaches Goals

Bob Zuppke, a famous football coach, once asked the question "What makes a man fight?" He answered his own question by saying: "Two forces are at war in every fighter, the ego and the goal. An over-dose of self-love, coddling of the ego, makes bums of men who ought to be champions. Forgetfulness of self, complete absorption in the goal, often makes champions out of bums."

Bob Zuppke talked about a football player as he sees a high punt sailing toward him. The player knows that if he catches that ball, some two hundred pounds of bone and muscle of an opposing player will hit him and hit him hard. He knows he may be hurt. But he really does not think of being hit or of being hurt. All he thinks of is that goal line that has to be crossed—has to be crossed—has to be crossed.

A goal that has to be crossed gives power and stamina to life. Admiral Robert Peary wrote: "The determination to reach the pole had become so much a part of my being that, strange as it may seem, I long ago ceased to think of myself save as an instrument for the attainment of that end."

The world laughed at the idea of a flying machine. But the Wright brothers did fly. An old man watched them work and listened to their talk. He said of them, "I knew as soon as I saw those boys that they were different from the folks down here. They had an idea. It possessed them. I used to listen as they argued by the hour. I didn't understand what they were driving at, but I understood them. I knew they would get there."

Pour out your own love, and it comes back to you in the form of power and strength. A middle-aged man lay dying, and he became mentally adjusted to it. In fact death seemed to him as a sweet relief from the heavy burdens of his life.

He told himself that others would carry on his business. A few close friends would miss him, but they would soon become adjusted to his death. Then he thought of his wife. He thought of how she loved him and how he loved her, of how they had worked and lived together. His death would break her heart. Suddenly he began saying, "I cannot do this to her. I must live for her sake." And live he did. Under the power of a love that would not let him go, new life became his.

A man did not have the money to go to school. But he did go! He carried a full course, met his classes, and did his studying. To make his way, he was a night watchman for four hours. He had only five hours a day to sleep. He ate only one meal a day, and he washed dishes in the cafeteria to pay for that one. For breakfast he would eat a bowl of cereal in his room. He skipped the other meal.

A person cannot live on only one good meal a day and five hours' sleep. But he did it for an entire year. Not only that, he thrived on it. How did he do it? He fixed his mind on a great goal. To reach that goal, he had to go to school. But he concentrated on the goal, and that sustained him.

When one finds himself being whipped by life, losing power and enthusiasm, the time has come to fix new goals—goals to which one can completely give oneself. What is your goal?

Recently I had cause to look up in my dictionary the word *enthusiasm*. My dictionary defined it as "keen, animated interest in and preoccupation with something." It doesn't say what the "something" has to be. It can be one of many things, but we have all observed that until one finds something to get excited about, he never really gets very far. Thinking of enthusiasm, I thought of seven things that it will do to us:

1. Enthusiasm Brings out Possibilities We Are Not Using.
All of us have seen an athletic team get excited and play "over their heads." The truth is they are not playing over their heads; what they have been doing is playing under their possibilities.

Through all the years of my ministry, I have used Adam Clark's commentary. This old commentary is not used by many people today, but I have found it to be of great benefit. Adam Clark mastered thirty languages during his lifetime. Once his schoolteacher told his father there was no need to keep Adam in school, that he was too dull and stupid to learn. Somehow Adam Clark got interested in reading the Bible. The Bible has a powerful effect on any person who reads it. It is different from any book or any literature that exists, and as he read the Bible he began to get enthusiastic about it. He wanted to learn more and more. It brought out his latent powers, and he became one of the great scholars of his day.

2. Enthusiasm Will Make Us Fight.
Many years ago I had the privilege of visiting personally with Gene Tunney. He at one time was the heavyweight boxing champion of the entire world. He beat the great Jack Dempsey. Visiting with him was for me a great experience. He told me of a time when he was in the navy

and felt he was just an ordinary sailor; but they began having boxing matches, and he got excited about boxing. Suddenly instead of being an ordinary sailor, he became a very enthusiastic person. He studied boxing, he trained, he worked, and he won the championship. Not every person can be a fighter like Gene Tunney, but every person will begin to fight in some way for some things when he gets excited enough about it.

3. Enthusiasm Will Make Us Work. No two people have the same talent. Some people can sing, some people have business acumen, some people have athletic abilities, and on and on. We see people every day who can do things that we cannot do. The important thing is getting excited about what we *can* do. I like the story of the little boy in school. The class was studying the multiplication table, and the teacher asked one boy to recite the nines. He was stumbling along, not doing too well. Finally he said, "Teacher, I do not know the nines very well, but I am a hound dog on the sevens." Now that boy appeals to me, and he is going to get somewhere. Enthusiasm gets me so excited about what I can do that I do not need to worry about what anybody else is doing. It takes away jealousy and resentments.

4. Enthusiasm Makes Me a Positive Person. Through the years of my ministry, I have watched people in the church. There are those who are critical of everything about it. On the other hand, I have seen people really get the Spirit of the Lord in their hearts, and they forget about their criticisms and begin to boost and build up. This applies to a town, a nation, your organization, and even to your own personal life. When you get enthusiastic, you forget even your own faults, and you begin to think of your powers.

5. Enthusiasm Makes Us Loyal to the Highest Things That We Believe in. When persons are enthusiastic, they want to do their best and be their best, and they begin looking to see what the best is. Enthusiasm creates lively interest, which leads to action.

6. *Enthusiasm Will Cause One to Pay the Price.* Most good things in life do not come cheaply. A price must be paid. Sometimes it is the sweat of our brows; sometimes it's working late in the night; sometimes it's giving ourselves to the highest and not being satisfied with anything less. There are two lines of a poem that I learned long ago that have both inspired me and haunted me. They are:

> Still as of old, men by themselves are priced—
> For thirty pieces Judas sold himself, not Christ.
>
> HESTER H. CHOLMONDELEY

7. *The Best Thing About Enthusiasm Is: It Will Make Us Pray.* We never pray until we have something to pray for. As long as we are all that we want to be, have everything we want to have, have done everything we want to do, then there is no need to pray. But when there is something out yonder to touch and we reach as far as we can, then we extend ourselves through the power of prayer.

Living in a world like this ought not to be a dull experience. Some of us need to get enthusiastic.

Relaxed Calmness

One of the greatest needs of people today is relaxed calmness.

Once there was a blacksmith putting a steel rim on the wheel of a wagon to be used on concrete pavement. Someone asked how long the blacksmith thought those steel rims would last. He replied that they were the finest quality of steel, and they ought to last at least for 3,000 miles. But the tires on your automobile will last for ten or even twenty times 3,000 miles. If you drove as slowly as that wagon went, your tires might even last 100,000 miles.

Comparing steel to rubber, it would seem that steel would last longer. The opposite is the case. Why? Because the steel is rigid and tense, but the rubber is relaxed and pliable. When the steel rim hits a rough place, it does not give; the rubber tire gives and takes according to the road over which it rolls.

One of the first things a boxer must learn is to "roll with the punches."

For many golfers, shooting across the water is a mental hazard. When a golfer stands on the tee and sees the water out in front, realizing he must drive across it, many times he will tense up and not hit his best shot. The professional golfer is never worried by a so-called waterhole because he concentrates on putting the ball on the green rather than fearing it might go into the water.

We concentrate on our difficulties, and we get tense and tight. Instead of thinking about the troubles we are facing, it is far better to look ahead to the brighter goals and happier days. J. Arthur Rank was a great motion-picture producer in Great Britain. When he went to his office, instead of using the elevator, he would walk up the stairs. He called them his prayer stairs. In the morning as he walked up he asked God to guide him in every decision and attitude that day. He would take each step separately and deliberately make it a part of his prayer. Then in the evening he would walk down slowly, thanking God for the help he had received that day.

He said those prayer steps did more than anything else to bring him a serene life.

FIVE

God Loves *YOU!*

One of the most marvelous stories in all the Bible is only one verse long. It can be read in just seconds, but it has a great lesson to teach people today. The story is: "Again, the kingdom of heaven is like unto treasure hid in a field; the which when a man hath found, he hideth, and for joy thereof goeth and selleth all that he hath, and buyeth that field" (Matthew 13:44).

Here was a tenant farmer; that was a hopeless, insecure position. A tenant could never hope to make enough money to ever buy a farm for himself. He rented the land from the owner, and they shared at the end of the year whatever the land had produced. More than likely, back at home there were underfed and underclothed children. Always he would face the possibility that at the end of the year the owner of the land would tell him to move on, that he was dissatisfied with his work on the farm.

Jesus tells about a tenant farmer who was ploughing in the field and found some buried treasure. Joyfully he went and sold all that he had and he bought that field, and the treasure and the field were his. From then on, he never had to share what he produced and he never heard anybody ever say, "Move on." For the first time he felt a sense of security. Even when he became old and unable to work, he could still live in his house and rent out his land to some other tenant farmer.

But look again at the story, which begins, ". . . the kingdom of heaven is. . . ." The point of the story is not the treasure hidden in the field; rather it is that a right relationship with God gives one a sense of inner security and peace. I can personally testify at this point. I grew up in small country towns in Georgia. When I was thirty-four years old, the largest town in which I had ever lived had a population of 3,000 people. One day the bishop of our church called and told me he wanted me to take a church in the center of Atlanta. I had never lived in a city, and I did not know how to deal with city people and city churches. We moved to Atlanta on Friday afternoon. On Saturday I went to look at the church sanctuary. I had never been inside that church before. As I walked into the sanctuary I felt completely overwhelmed. I certainly did not feel adequate for that church. After a while I knelt at the altar and I prayed that day for God's help in a way that I had never prayed before.

When I left that altar I had a calmness and a peace that I have never lost since then. I have made mistakes and blunders, but somehow I have never felt worried, and I have always had a sense of the adequacy of God. I remained as the pastor of Grace United Methodist Church in Atlanta for twelve years. It was a happy, exciting experience. Every Sunday night during those twelve years, at the close of my sermon, I would invite the people to come and pray at the altar. The church was always filled with people, and hundreds of those people would line up in the aisles to kneel at that sacred place.

Through the years of life, I have learned that not only does God help you and make up for your insufficiencies, but also there are always people who will help you. I know some people will criticize and condemn, but there are more people who will compliment and support and build up. When we do our best, we

can be sure that not only will God be for us, but most people will
be for us, also.

Nothing Can Defeat You

When I name my favorite chapters of the Bible, I never forget
Romans 8. That to me is one of the inspirational peaks in all literature. A lot of people go through life defeated; they struggle,
hoping that some day they will gain a victory, but the victory
seems to never come. After a while, they lose hope. They become
resigned to their fate. All the wonders of life are for somebody
else.

Saint Paul wrote to the early Christians of Rome. They lived in
the greatest city of the entire world, but the people of that city
had become drunk with their own position and power. Day by
day, they saw the mighty armies of Caesar; they felt their society
would live forever. Caesar had brought them luxury and wealth,
fame and power, security and satisfaction. When people reach the
point at which they do not need God, they seem to lose God.
These Romans became morally corrupt, godless people. They
had Caesar, they had no need for any other god. Their sport was
persecuting the Christians. They would shout encouragement to
the lions who were about to tear the Christians to pieces, limb by
limb. The homes of the Christians were burned, with everything
they owned in them, while the owners were forced to stand helplessly by. For the Christians in Rome every day might be the last
day. No wonder many of them felt hopelessly defeated.

To these people Saint Paul wrote this letter to the Romans.
They would meet secretly together, and one would read aloud the
words of this matchless preacher. Reading this letter would so
charge them with faith that they could go out and face anything
undaunted or unafraid. The one thing Saint Paul was saying to
them, above all things, was, "Remember—nothing can defeat
you."

The other day I was in an airplane flying across the Rocky Mountains. My eyes were glued to the wonderful and beautiful scenery. Everywhere you looked, you felt inspiration. However, as we flew across the Rockies, the one thing I was looking for above all things was Pike's Peak. So it is with the Book of Romans; it is thrilling all the way through, but somehow to me the eighth chapter is the Pike's Peak.

Paul states the basis for the hope the Romans had in the first verse of the chapter: "There is therefore now no condemnation to them which are in Christ Jesus, who walk not after the flesh, but after the Spirit."

I always pause and rejoice when I come to the fifteenth verse of this eighth chapter. Read with me again these words: "For ye have not received the spirit of bondage again to fear; but ye have received the Spirit of adoption, whereby we cry, Abba, Father."

I can imagine how these early Christians felt when they read the eighteenth verse and how encouraged they were. We have had sufferings, we have had loved ones die, we have had physical illness, we have had hurts and disappointments, but isn't it wonderful to read: "For I reckon that the sufferings of this present time are not worthy to be compared with the glory which shall be revealed in us."

When I feel as if the clouds have obscured the sunshine of life and there isn't much more to live for, I always remember Saint Paul said these words: "For we are saved by hope: but hope that is seen is not hope: for what a man seeth, why doth he yet hope for? But if we hope for that we see not, then do we with patience wait for it" (verses 24, 25). When it seems as if the clouds have blotted out the sunshine of life and that everything is lost, it is thrilling to realize we can still cling to our hope and that hope will save us, and out of that hope we gain patience.

Then we come to the twenty-eighth verse. Across the years, this has been one of the favorite texts of my sermons. Over and over, I have preached to people these marvelous words, "And we know that all things work together for good to them that love God, to them who are the called according to his purpose."

That verse reminds me of a ship. The business of a ship is to sail across the sea. However, if you lay the engine of the ship on the water, it will sink. The same is true of the propeller, or even the compass that guides the ship. In fact, you can take off almost any part of the ship and put it on the water, and it will sink. But if all the parts of the ship are built securely together, then the ship will sail through even the worst storm.

Life is like that. Many things that happen in life are not good. Bad things do happen to good people. The truth is we are all good as long as things are going well. However, there are many times when things are not going well, when they are tragic and heartbreaking, and they are painful. Saint Paul did not say that everything that happens is good. What he said is, if you will take all the experiences of life, cement them together with your love for God, then we can be sure that everything will work out well. In the long run God is not going to let His children be defeated.

Reading the eighth chapter of the Book of Romans, I sometimes find myself hurrying to get to the climax. I remember when I was a little boy and mama would fix dinner; she would often have one of her wonderful home-baked pies for dessert. Having seen the pie and knowing it was there, sometimes I hurried through dinner because I wanted the dessert. And what a marvelous climax we read here! Let me quote here these words:

Who shall separate us from the love of Christ? shall tribulation, or distress, or persecution, or famine, or nakedness, or peril, or sword? As it is written, For thy sake we are killed all the day long; we are accounted as sheep for the slaughter. Nay, in all these things we are more than conquerors through him that loved us. For I am persuaded, that neither death, nor life, nor angels, nor principalities, nor powers, nor things present, nor things to come. Nor height, nor depth, nor any other creature, shall be able to separate us from the love of God, which is in Christ Jesus our Lord.

Romans 8:35–39

Truly those words are one of the Pike's Peaks of not only the Bible, but of all literature throughout the ages. It says to us that, in spite of the very worst things that might happen to us, we have the assurance that nothing, absolutely nothing, can separate us from the love of God. And having the assurance that we have God's love, we can go on to victory.

Never forget the Christian gospel can be summed up in three words: *God loves you.*

How different each and every one of us would be if we could plant deeply in our minds those words "in all things"—what things?—*all things*—we are more than conquerors.

Let each of us ask the question: What am I facing that might defeat me? sickness? financial troubles? loneliness? fear of some kind? a general state of unhappiness? a feeling there is nothing to live for? trouble in reference to my job? some person I love is in trouble? the feeling of inadequacy?

Saint Paul did not say we could defeat some things. He said we can conquer "all these things." Let's go back and read some of these words again: "no condemnation." That is, no matter what you might have done or not have done, the past is past; you need not condemn yourself. We can get rid of our scorching memories.

"Saved by hope"—hope looks to tomorrow. You never hope looking backwards. Thinking about past defeats never saved anybody.

"All things ... for good"—not just some things. Everything that happens can be blended in together and worked out with a good ending.

"Separate us from the love of Christ"—this is the height of all living; when we know that God loves us, then we are never defeated. When we plant deeply into our minds these glorious and victorious thoughts that we find in the eighth chapter of the Book of Romans, then we realize nothing—nothing—can defeat us. "We are more than conquerors."

Someone asked me recently how many times I had been to the Holy Land. I had to stop and count before I could answer, "Twenty-two times." Then my friend said, "What do you plan to do after you retire from the active ministry?" I replied that I had several things in mind, but I intended the major activity of my life to be going to the Holy Land. I love to go there, and now it's for me a very happy and wonderful experience. I know the people and the hotels, even the waiters and the busboys and the cleaning people, and they all call me by name. I know the bus drivers and guides and the people in so many places where we stop. And now going back to the Holy Land is sort of an old-home week for me. However, the most compelling reason for going back to the Holy Land is the difference I see in the lives of people who go with me. I like to have a fairly good-sized group of people. Too small a group is not as happy as a larger group. Each night, after dinner, it is a thrilling thing for us to gather together in a special room the hotel provides for us and sing the old songs about Jesus; then I talk about His life. Somehow He seems more real then than at any other time.

I like to stand and look over the shepherd fields. Those fields are the same today as they were 2,000 years ago. Nothing has been built in those fields, and the sheep are out there grazing now just as they used to. We stand there together, and I quote the words of the second chapter of Saint Luke's Gospel, beginning with the eighth verse, "And there were in the same country shepherds abiding in the field, keeping watch over their flock by night." After we have heard the story recorded there, we sing some of the beautiful Christmas carols, always closing with "Silent night! holy night! All is calm, all is bright." Somehow the birth of Jesus means more in that moment than you can ever imagine.

One of the places I like to go the most is Nazareth. Walking around Nazareth, I know there are more people living there now, and I know there are more buildings there. On the other hand, I know that is the same ground where Jesus walked as a little boy and where He grew up to be a thirty-year-old man. I keep wondering why the story of Jesus has lasted this long. Why do people still want to see Jacob's well and the town where Jesus healed the lepers and the mountain where the Transfiguration took place and the Sea of Galilee upon which He walked and the place Jesus was when the little boy gave Him his loaves and fishes and He multiplied and fed the multitude? And Jericho and the Jordan River. In Israel I like to stay in a beautiful hotel on the Mount of Olives. Perhaps the highlight of the entire trip is having Holy Communion in a lovely little amphitheater out in front of the hotel. I have a friend in Israel who makes for me some little cups out of olive wood. I tell the people that after they have taken communion, they may keep their little cups as a precious remembrance.

Sitting there, we can see the place where the Upper Room was and the valley through which He and His disciples walked to the Garden of Gethsemane, just below where we are. We can see where the dungeon was where He was put that night, after He had been scourged, and we can see the streets of Jerusalem through which He walked and bore His cross. Just beyond the city are Calvary's hill and the garden tomb. Of course, no one knows for sure where He was crucified and buried, but that place seems so like what I have always imagined it to be that now I have come to believe it is the place. I walk into that tomb, and I see again that it is empty. As I leave the Holy Land it always overwhelms me when I realize that the life of that one person who lived in that little land has been the most influential life ever lived on this earth. After 2,000 years millions of people worship Him. There is no way to explain it in human terms. There is something different about Him from any person who ever lived on this earth.

As little children we learn to sing:

> Jesus loves me! this I know,
> For the Bible tells me so.

Later on in the hard press of life, many of us have been able to sing:

> Jesus calls us o'er the tumult
> Of our life's wild, restless sea.

Millions of people respond to that call.

Then, as the latter years of life come upon us, when the shadows have lengthened and we have seen some of the pain and harshness of life, just as eagerly as when we were little children, we sing again:

> Jesus, lover of my soul,
> Let me to thy bosom fly.

Through the years of my ministry, I have spoken many, many times at banquets and conventions of all types. I can tell a joke, and people will laugh; I can talk about the happenings of the day, and people are interested. When I begin to talk about Jesus, I see faces grow softer, and many times eyes become misty. People are strangely fascinated by Jesus.

I read about an aviator who was flying across the Black Hills of South Dakota when suddenly he came upon that beautifully impressive carving of four great Americans, standing there in all its beauty on the rocks of one of those hills. He saw the faces of Washington, Lincoln, Jefferson, and Theodore Roosevelt. He was so fascinated by those faces that he circled several times just to look upon them.

Something like that happens to people flying along through life—through sunshine and clouds. One day—it may be during the service in a church; it may be through some act of love and kindness of a friend; it may be as one is reading the Bible; it may be in some moment of quietness, but some time we see His face, and we are captivated by it. Forever afterwards, life is different for us.

One historian has said of Him, "When the final history of mankind has been written, its proudest glory would be that there once walked into ancient Jerusalem and into the hearts of mankind a simple peasant named Jesus of Nazareth."

Once you have been to the land where He lived, you can understand why I enjoy going so much and intend to go several times a year as long as I am physically able.

Very simply Jesus told people to "love one another." Hearing that, one can imagine how some of those Roman soldiers must have convulsed with laughter. They thought the way to win in this life was to have the greatest physical force.

He said, "Heaven and earth shall pass away: but my words shall not pass away" (Mark 13:31). People who heard that must have thought, *How stupid that is. This unknown peasant thinking that as long as civilization lives, people will be quoting His words.* Today, the mighty armies of proud Rome have passed away, but not the words that He spoke.

He said, ". . . I go to prepare a place for you" (John 14:2). There comes a time when that means more to us than any words that have ever been spoken. We buy land on this earth, we build houses, but we know that our existence here is temporary. There comes a day when we become more interested in the place that

He was talking about. One of the highlight experiences that I have had came one day when I was working in my study at the church in Atlanta. My phone rang and the voice said, "Charles, this is Frank Laubach." When I think of the Christians that have lived on this earth, one of the names I remember is Frank C. Laubach. His little book *Prayer, the Mightiest Force in the World,* has been one of the inspirations of my life. I was young in the ministry at that time, and I just could not believe that the great Dr. Laubach was calling me. He said, "I want to come out and visit with you." We sat together—I do not know how long—I was so fascinated by him that time made no difference. He was not a large man, physically; he was a rather quiet and unassuming person. There was about him a gentlenesss that was almost fragile. Finally the time came for him to leave, and he said to me, "Charles, let's you and I pray together."

We stood up, we joined hands, he closed his eyes and looked up toward the ceiling. I never shall forget his first sentence, he said, "O Jesus Christ, I can see you right now, and I am so glad that you are smiling."

It is a marvelous thing to realize that we have a Christ who is smiling. He isn't angry with us: He is smiling.

She Asked for It, and She Got It

People of my generation remember Jane Froman, a wonderful singer. In college she wanted to attend an opera in Saint Louis. She had no way to get there; in spite of that, she went to the dean and asked permission to go. He smiled and said to her that he and his wife were going, and they would be delighted to have her go with them. She asked for it, and she got it.

During the Second World War, she was in a plane wreck in Lisbon, Portugal. Badly broken in body and in spirit, Jane wanted to return home, but absolutely no transportation was available. She wrote a simple letter to President Franklin D. Roosevelt and asked him to help her. She barely had time to pack her belongings to take advantage of the seat on the plane the president had made available to her. She asked for it, and she got it.

Back home in the United States, Jane needed a car; this was immediately after the war, and friends reminded her that getting a car was impossible. Thousands of people were waiting for the cars they had ordered. Some were even paying substantial amounts of money over the list price of the car to get one. Jane Froman simply looked up the name of the president of an automobile company; she had never heard of him before. She wrote him a simple letter and asked for a car. He answered her with a very short letter; in fact, he only asked her one question: What color did she want? She asked for it, and she got it.

Some people smile at stories like that, but Jesus taught that principle long, long ago. He said, "Ask, and it shall be given you ... For every one that asketh receiveth" (Matthew 7:7, 8). Jesus also said, "And all things, whatsoever ye shall ask in prayer, believing, ye shall receive" (Matthew 21:22).

He said, "And whatsoever ye shall ask in my name, that will I do ..." (John 14:13). James summed it all up when he said, "... Ye have not, because ye ask not" (James 4:2). At this point we need to underscore four important principles:

1. Decide What You Really Want. Be clear and definite. Think of your mind as a motion picture screen; flash on that screen the picture of what you are asking for. Take it off, put it on, take it off, put it on, until that picture becomes sharp and clear, until you know definitely what you want. The tragedy of so many people is they do not know what to ask for.

After you get that picture clearly before you, then test it. Is it good for you? Is it fair to all others concerned? Are you ready for it now? Do you honestly feel that it is according to God's will?

If after testing your desire, you are ready to go to God with it, then do not hesitate.

2. Ask Believing.   Jesus said, "And all things, whatsoever ye shall ask in prayer, believing, ye shall receive" (Matthew 21:22). Underscore that word *believing*. It means to be hopeful, optimistic, to know that it is possible. One of the stumbling blocks of people is, "Lord, You wouldn't do this for me." You have to believe that God would do it.

3. Begin Doing What You Can to Get What You Have Asked For.   I know a girl who went to work in a large company as a clerk typist. One day she asked her boss for a raise. He explained to her that he was paying her as much as any of the other people in her category. If she wanted more money, then she needed to qualify for it. She found a business school and enrolled for night courses. She studied, developed her skills, increased her knowledge, and she received far more than she asked for and even more than she had ever dreamed of making. Just wanting something is not enough. Doing something about it helps a great deal, and the truth is, asking God for something is our greatest inspiration for getting up and beginning to do something. God gives us more than we ever dream He can give us. But He begins by giving us inspiration only when we are ready to receive it.

4. Know That God Wants the Very Best for You.   Read carefully these words: "If ye then, being evil, know how to give good gifts unto your children, how much more shall your Father which is in heaven give good things to them that ask him?" (Matthew 7:11).

Truly we want the best for our children. Therefore it is not hard for us to picture in our minds a heavenly Father who knows and loves us and wants the best for us. Concentrate on the goodness of God.

I know about a church who got a new minister. Later someone asked one of the members of the church how he liked the new minister. He replied, "He is the greatest minister we ever had. In fact he asks God for things that our last preacher didn't even know the Lord had."

SIX

Believe in Yourself

Who is the most interesting person in the world?

If you want to find the answer to that question, I can tell you how to do it. Go on a picnic with a group of people, have a camera with you, and take snapshots of various groups. Then select certain persons and show them the snapshots you took. If you watch carefully, you will notice they spend most of the time looking at the pictures in which they themselves are included. People like to look at themselves. The most interesting person in the world is you, yourself. So one of the things I like to say to people is, Do not be ashamed to be yourself.

Robert Louis Stevenson said, "To be what we are, and to become what we are capable of becoming, is the only end of life." Yet one of the major causes of unhappiness is that we are dissatisfied with ourselves. If you meet a twelve-year-old boy and say to him, "Why, my little man, you look big enough to be fourteen years old," you have made a friend for life.

A clerk in a store told me that a number of times he has had a mother and daughter come into his department to buy a dress. Often the daughter would buy a dress, and then he would say, "Would your sister also like to buy a dress?" He told me that that question always got a good response.

If you see a young medical student in a hospital and say to that student, "Doctor, can you tell me where this room is located?" he will straighten up and beam with pride.

A friend told me that when you are stopped by a traffic cop, never forget the first word to say is *captain.* No traffic cop ever resents being called captain.

A friend told me that many times you can say to a minister, "After listening to your sermon this morning, I thought what a great lawyer you could have been." My friend said that many ministers straighten up and say, "Well, I did think once of taking up the law."

There exists in all of us a tendency to pretend we are something other than what we are. This can be good if it inspires us, but it may also reach the point where it makes us miserable.

We need to remember that everything God made on this earth has its own separate identity. No two snowflakes have ever been identical. No two blades of grass are the same, and no person who ever lived or ever will live is exactly like me or you. Our bodies are different; the prints of our fingers are different; we think differently; and each of us can do something that no other person who ever lived can do. You can make some contribution in life, and if you do not make it, then it will never be made. Among the more than 4 billion people on earth, there is only one me and only one you.

One day a sixth-grade teacher asked her class this question: "What is here in the world today that was not here fifteen years ago?" She expected them to tell of some new invention or discovery. One little boy held up his hand. "All right, Johnny, what is here that was not here fifteen years ago?" He replied, "Me." And that little boy is right.

When you believe that you are a person that God created, it does two things for you:

1. It rids you of the jealousy in your heart. Jealousy breeds hate, prejudice, greed, and all the other destructive emotions. It

makes a person miserable. Envy will cause a person to be unhappy when someone else receives an honor or a blessing. Because of this attitude a person will be secretly glad when someone
else is hurt. An inferiority complex comes as a result of your
being ashamed to be yourself.

2. When you come to the point that you are willing to be yourself, then you get busy on yourself. You are the one person you
can take responsibility for. You love your parents, and you love
your children, but you can lay claim to their lives only to a point.
However, you can be much more responsible for your own life.
There is no reason to be unhappy over past failures. When you
have a reason for living, you look toward the future. You climb
toward that goal. Even though you may have failed, if you
sincerely try and give your best, your heart contains a glow and a
zest and a happiness. Anticipation is one of the greatest inspirations in living.

There is marvelous power in asking ourselves, "Why did God
make me?" The answer to that question provides one of the greatest inspirations for living. As we begin giving ourselves to the
purpose for which we were born we grow and develop and find
our highest place in life. We begin to realize the exhilarating
thought *This world is better because I am living in it.*

We Want to Feel Important

Once someone asked three great psychologists this question,
"What is the one thing people want more than anything else?"
Those three psychologists gave their answers.

Freud said, "The one thing people want the most is to be
loved."

Jung said, "To be secure is what people want the most."

Adler said, "They want most to feel important."

I agree with Adler. More than being loved or being secure, we want to feel that we amount to something. One great obstacle in the way of our feeling important is our feeling of unimportance. We want to feel superior, but many of us feel inferior. In some way nearly every person has an inferiority complex. A feeling of inferiority is a very serious enemy in our lives. It must be faced and overcome.

Here let me list six wrong methods of trying to overcome an inferiority complex:

1. The Superiority Smoke-Screen Method. A person may feel miserably inferior and in an effort to hide it become abnormally aggressive, boastful, dictatorial. Many try to hide an inferiority with a show of superiority. We see it in the child saying, "Look how high I can jump," or in the loud dresser, the big talker, profuse jewelry, and overdressing. We see it in people who become hysterical and in others who become emotionally drunk.

2. The Sour-Grapes Method. We are all familiar with Aesop's fable of the fox and the sour grapes. He jumped and jumped, and when he realized he couldn't reach the grapes, he concluded they were sour and not worth reaching. The frail youth discounts athletics. The dumb person laughs at intellectual highbrows; the morally degenerate scoffs at ideals.

3. The Daydreaming Method. To some extent all of us live in a world of fantasy. That is not bad; in fact, it is normal and right. If we never fantasized, we would never see ourselves as better than we are. To fantasize our dreams can be a very blessed experience. On the other hand, being unable to face the real world, we can retreat entirely into the world of fantasy.

Charles A. Lindbergh dreamed of flying across the Atlantic Ocean, but he was not willing to be satisfied with just his dreams.

He had to get in an airplane and take off. So it is with us; it is a tragedy when we satisfy our ambitions with our dreams.

I like the spirit of the one who said, "I would rather be a good ditch digger than dream of building Panama Canals and never do anything."

4. The Excuse Method. In Matthew 25:14–30 Jesus told a story about a man who was to make a journey into a far country. He called three of his servants together and gave them resources. We read, "And unto one he gave five talents, to another two, and to another one. . . ." Then he went on his journey. While he was gone we read, "He that had received the five talents went and traded with the same, and made them other five talents. And like-wise he that had received two, he also gained other two. But he that had received one went and digged in the earth, and hid his lord's money."

Finally the man returned home, and he called for an account-ing. We find the servant who received five talents doubled his; also the man who received two talents doubled his; but the third man who had received one talent said, "And I was afraid, and went and hid thy talent in the earth. . . ." He did not use the talent he received. Why was he afraid? He blamed it on the master. He said that he knew that the master was a hard man and difficult to satisfy. The truth is, he was afraid that he could not make as big a showing as the others made. He was afraid that he would look bad by comparison. That is the reason a lot of us do not use the talents and opportunities we have, but we never admit it to our-selves. Instead we make excuses and use them as a convenient escape.

5. The Extreme Sensitivity Method. Oftentimes you can tell the size of a person by what upsets him or her. Some people have an almost insane desire for attention, and if they do not get it, they become very unhappy. These people might say, "I went to church, and nobody spoke to me." The self-confident person does not wait for somebody else to speak. The self-confident person is not worried about being passed by. Defeated people get so touchy and get their feelings hurt.

6. The Highly Critical Method. People like this may gossip about their neighbors. Feeling little themselves, they whittle us all down to their own size. They minister to their own conceits by picking out flaws in other people.

These six methods never succeed; in fact they make the problem worse.

It is altogether right to desire to feel that you amount to something. We all want to feel accepted by other people, and we want to be able to accept ourselves. That rightful desire must be directed into constructive channels. Here let us consider four ways by which one can overcome a feeling of unimportance or inferiority—four ways that are good and will work.

1. Recognize That You Are Needed in the World. Some time ago I was driving on a country road. I came to a crossroad, and there was no sign there to indicate the way. I did not know which way to go. Nearby was a small store. I stopped there, before four men sitting out front. I asked them which was the right way, and all four started talking at the same time. They helped me, but also I helped them. Every cry for help is a stimulating experience.

The greatest dream and ambition in Saint Paul's life was to go to Bithynia. Instead he landed in lowly Troas. He was a broken and defeated man. Then we read, "And a vision appeared to Paul in the night; There stood a man of Macedonia, and prayed him, saying, Come over into Macedonia, and help us" (Acts 16:9). That call for help was the turning point in Saint Paul's ministry. It saved him from despair.

Consider an ordinary piece of telephone wire. It is made of

common materials and is not especially valuable. However if you use that wire to carry a message of supreme importance, then it becomes notable because it has served a key purpose.

Here is a bucket. That bucket is not particularly precious, but suppose it is used to carry water to one who is dying of thirst. Then that bucket becomes more valuable than gold. It has been used in the saving of a life.

Stradivari had an ambition to play the violin, but he did not have the talent to do it. Instead he became a maker of violins. George Eliot wrote of him these words:

> When any master holds
> 'Twixt chin and hand a violin of mine,
> He will be glad that Stradivari lived,
> Made violins, and made them of the best.
> The masters only know whose work is good;
> They will choose mine, while God gives them skill,
> I give them the instruments to play upon
> God choosing me to help Him.

Service is one of the surest ways to not only feel important, but to be important.

2. Realize Your Possibilities and Realize You Are Important. A little six-week-old baby and a six-week-old puppy dog sit on the floor together. Watching them, one might conclude that the little puppy dog is much the superior. The little dog can run around by itself, can drink water, and has even begun to eat its food. If you call to the little puppy dog, it will probably respond.

On the other hand, the six-week-old baby can only lie on the floor. It cannot crawl or service itself in any way.

Looking at those two when they are six weeks old, it is very easy to get a false impression. When you think about what those two will become, then you see the vast difference. The little puppy dog and the little baby have entirely different futures. That little baby is a human being, a person, a child of God.

When the puppy dog is buried in the ground, that is the end of it; but when that little baby reaches the end of life on this earth, it has an eternity to live.

There is a vast difference between an animal and a person—especially when you look at what they might become.

3. Stand for Something Greater Than Yourself. A charm school taught each student to stand before a large mirror and repeat her name in a soft voice, gentle and low, so as to impress herself with herself.

That type of teaching produces characters like a girl named Edith. It was said, "Edith is a little country, bounded on the north by Edith, and on the south by Edith, and on the east by Edith, and on the west by Edith."

A hospital nurse had a patient who was very disagreeable to work with. She could hardly bear to enter that room. She was about to quit when into her mind came these words, ". . . Inasmuch as ye have done it unto one of the least of these my brethren, ye have done it unto me" (Matthew 25:40). She realized that even the most disagreeable task can be part of a great cause, and that gave her the courage to go on.

Let us think of two rooms. The walls of one are lined with mirrors. One can stand anywhere in the room and look in any direction and see oneself. The walls of the other room are made up of windows. Standing in that room, one might look in every direction and see the great and glorious world. There are great and majestic trees, green grass, lovely flowers, rolling hills, the sky, the rain, the sunshine, and all the glories of the world. It is exciting to realize the world in which we are living.

It makes a lot of difference in one's attitude toward oneself, whether that person lives in a room of mirrors or a room of windows.

4. Cultivate a Sense of Belonging to God.   Someone once said to another man, "Why don't you admit that you are inferior?" The man made a wonderful reply: "I am a child of God, and out of loyalty to my Father, I cannot admit that."

A boy made a little boat. Carefully he carved the wood and put the pieces together. On it he put a beautiful little sail. He took his boat down to the lake to let it sail along the shore. A gust of wind came and carried the little boat out across the water, beyond his reach. His little boat was gone, and for days he looked for it but could never find it. Then one day in the window of a store he saw his little boat for sale. On it was a price tag of one dollar. He ran home and got his bank, in which he had some money. He took out a dollar, went back to the store, and bought the little boat.

As he was walking home, holding the little boat in his arms, he said, "Little boat, little boat, you are mine, all mine. I made you and I bought you." That is what God says about each one of us. He made us, and with the life of His Son He bought us. We are God's persons.

Learn How to Leave

One of life's finest lessons is to learn how to leave.

Life is a journey. If you go someplace, you must leave some other place. You cannot both go and stay. For example if you are in Chicago and want to go to New York, you have to leave Chicago before you can go to New York. So it is with life experiences. We are compelled to leave some experiences in order to have others. Jesus told some people, "Remember Lot's wife!" (Luke 17:32). It would be good for all of us to remember Lot's wife. With her family they were in one city; they felt the call to move to another area. On the road she stopped and looked back. She did not want to leave, even though she wanted the other place. The result was that in stopping she became a pillar of salt. You read this story in the nineteenth chapter of the Book of Genesis, and it is a story that has meaning for each and every one of us. She wanted tomorrow, but she also wanted to hold on to yesterday.

At the time I am writing these words, I am in my twenty-third year as the pastor of a church in the very center of the downtown section of Houston, Texas. During these twenty-three years, the population of Houston has greatly increased. People have moved to this city from all over the world. I have come to know a lot of these individuals, and I say that many of them are very miserable because they never learned how to move. I came to Houston from Atlanta, Georgia; I loved Georgia and will love it until I die. I was born there, and my parents and their parents were born there. I met my wife in Georgia, and my children were born there. We moved to Houston the first of September; in November someone said to me, "Are you going back home for Christmas?" I replied, "I am at home now." The day we drove into this city, it was our home. A lot of people have never learned that lesson. When you live in one place and think of home as "back yonder, some other place," you are in for a lot of misery.

A sea captain once said, "Even if I am in port for only one day, I always let my anchor down." Jesus had something to say along this line. He was talking to people who looked back with futile regret at the things they left behind. "No man, having put his hand to the plough, and looking back, is fit for the kingdom of God" (Luke 9:62).

When we constantly think of the past, our minds play tricks on us. For example, we can have a picnic, it rains, ants get in the food, mosquitoes bite us, and it is hot and humid. But a year later, we look back and forget about the rain and the ants and the mosquitoes and the hot sun, and somehow we remember what a beautiful experience the picnic was.

So it is with our experiences in life. There is a tendency to glorify the past. We hear people talk about "the good old days." The truth is, the old days were never as good as people remember them as being.

We need to learn how to leave some of our unhappy experiences. From year to year I look forward to Thanksgiving Day. At this marvelous time in the life of our nation, we are reminded to be thankful for our blessings. On Thanksgiving Day I often think about those hearty and wonderful pilgrims who celebrated the first Thanksgiving Day. Half their company had died that year; they had barely been able to grow enough food to keep them alive. Savages were lurking all about them; they had very poor places to live. In spite of that they set aside a day for thanksgiving.

SEVEN
The Changing Power of Prayer

I have counseled many people that they need to learn from the mistakes they have made, the wrongs they have done, the sins they have committed. God never completely wipes out our memories. However God can flood those memories with His forgiving grace. He can transform our wounds, our mistakes, our sins into sources of strength. God leaves us with the memories of our past, but takes away the control the past has over us. The remembrance of some things humbles us, but because of God's forgiving grace, they no longer humiliate us.

Through the years I have been blessed with the reading of the works of Henry Drummond, who wrote the finest interpretation of the thirteenth chapter of 1 Corinthians. Someone asked Mr. Drummond what had been the greatest influence in his life. He replied, "Ten minutes every day in the company of Christ, aye, two minutes thus spent every day will make the whole day different."

He did not say that we must pray all night. He did not even say we must pray for an hour. First he said ten minutes, but quickly changed that to just two minutes. Two minutes is not a long time, but two minutes consciously spent in a spiritual way can be a tremendous life-changing experience.

My oldest brother, Stanley F. Allen, and I took our vacations together for many years. One of the places we enjoyed being in the most was the Highlands Country Club in Highlands, North Carolina. We spent many, many weeks in that beautiful place. One day we were sitting on the porch of the country-club hotel. He was reading the newspaper, greatly concerned with the weather report. In Mississippi it was raining, and he was worried because he was a farmer. He was also the business manager of a college and a banker, and I used to accuse him of working at those jobs so he would have money enough to run his farm. On that vacation he told me that if the rain didn't stop, his crop would be wiped out.

My brother was always a religious man and a leader in the church. So I told him, "Why don't you pray about it?" He expressed some rather strong thoughts, saying he did not believe praying would have much effect on the weather in Mississippi. He followed it with some comments about us "impractical preachers." But we continued talking and came to the conclusion that maybe praying would not affect the rain in Mississippi, but it would tremendously affect his attitude toward it. He accepted that, and after praying, we went out that day and had one of the most enjoyable games of golf we had ever had.

Maybe spending time in the presence of Christ, through prayer and meditation, will not affect the rain in Mississippi or the circumstances in my life, but it will affect me and my spirit, and it will give me the serene poise to accept the rain or whatever comes.

One of the most marvelous promises that ever fell from the lips of Jesus Christ are these words, "If ye abide in me, and my words abide in you, ye shall ask what ye will, and it shall be done unto you" (John 15:7). What does it mean to abide in Jesus? It means to think about Him, to let Him possess our minds. Through the years I have developed some simple, but effective techniques. I can imagine various scenes in His life and sort of relive them. Since I have been going to the land where He lived, this is even easier for me. There is a song "I Walked Today Where Jesus Walked," and when one has literally done that, Jesus seems even closer.

I like to watch Him, in my mind, as the little children come. I can see Him sitting down, with one of the children sitting on His lap, another standing by His side, and others sitting all around Him. I can imagine His smile, expressions of His love, His friendly spirit. Sitting there with those little children, I feel real close to Jesus.

I enjoy spending time with the hungry multitude that day. I think about being hungry, and then I watch as He takes the little boy's lunch, the loaves and the fishes, and begins to break them. I watch as the disciples pass out the food. In my mind I reach for some fish and a loaf, and I begin to eat. Being there in that setting is an inspiring experience for me.

Most I enjoy riding with Him on the boat on the Sea of Galilee. Each time I go to Israel with a group of people, we plan to ride across that lovely little sea. I know the captain of the boat and the people who operate it, so when we get out in the middle, I ask him to stop the engines for a few moments. Then I read that Bible story about Jesus stilling the tempest. I talk a little about the story and about the tempest in our own lives, and then we have prayer. That really is one of the high moments of the entire trip to the Holy Land. But here in my own room I sometimes, through the marvelous power of imagination, picture myself on that boat. I hear Him saying, "Peace, be still." When I feel bothered and upset and agitated, it is marvelous to feel the stormy waters within my own heart and mind being stilled. Then I can go on with my work.

Many times I have knelt at Gethsemane, where He prayed, and

many times as I go about my daily life, when I feel uncertain in reference to some decision, I like to just stop for two minutes and kneel with Him and say, ". . . Nevertheless, not my will, but thine, be done" (Luke 22:42).

I have come to love those little two-minute visits with Jesus in the various experiences of His life, and always I find inspiration.

We need to remind ourselves that Jesus is real. My father is real, but he is not physically present. My mother is real, but neither is she present. My two brothers are real, but they are both in another life. Even my own wife is as real to me as she has ever been, yet she, too, is in the Father's House. These whom I have loved so much do not have to be physically present in order for me to have fellowship with them. So it is with the Lord Jesus Christ. I know that He is not here physically, but I also know that I can have fellowship with Him, and even if I spend only two minutes in His presence, I feel inspired and lifted up.

Suppose you are worried or downhearted or disturbed; suddenly standing by your side is Jesus Christ in the physical flesh. You hear Him saying, "Son [or daughter] I know and I understand. You have something hard to face this day [or this week, or this month, or this year]. I want you to know that I am right here with you, and you and I will be facing it together." If you had that experience, you would not then be afraid of anything; it would change your personality.

Just two minutes every day!

Faith Never Fails

More than thirty years ago, Pat O'Brien wrote an article in a magazine that has inspired me and millions of others through the year: *Guideposts.* The article told about his own faith. Pat O'Brien is a great movie actor, but he also is a great person. In that article he told about a time when his daughter was very sick and suddenly, as if touched by the hand of God, the child became well. His wife noticed the miracle and rushed into the room where he was to tell him the good news. She found Pat praying. He said, "There was nothing else I could do."

Mrs. O'Brien simply replied, "Nothing else was needed."

He closed that article with these words:

> Faith never fails. Like an illimitable reserve fund, it is always waiting to give protection, inspiration, forgiveness, courageous and spiritual joy. I am firmly convinced that anything I am today and everything I have today, I owe to my faith. . . . I can ask no greater thrill in life than sitting in church on Sunday with my treasured mother, my beloved life partner, Eloise, and my four youngsters, all understanding and trying hard to serve God.

Years ago I used to read the writings of Dr. Alexis Carrel. In my notes I have this quotation from him: "Prayer is not only worship, it is an invisible emanation of man's spirit, the most powerful form of energy that can be generated."

This great scientist went on to say, "The influence of prayer on the human mind is as demonstrable as that of secreting glands. As a physician I have seen men, after all other therapy has failed, lifted out of disease and melancholy, by the supreme effort of prayer. It is the only power in the world that seems to overcome the so-called laws of nature."

A few days ago I was in a group that sang Irving Berlin's wonderful hymn, "God Bless America." When I sing that hymn, I always think of Kate Smith, who uniquely charmed our nation with her singing. One radio program of hers made a profound impression upon me. Ted Collins, her business manager, had had a heart attack and was gravely ill. There was real doubt as to whether or not he would live. On that particular radio program, Kate Smith talked about prayer. She told about an experience in a beauty parlor. A spark flew out of the hand dryer and set afire the cotton wadding around her head. Her hair was burned off, her eyebrows were burned away, and her face and arms were burned. The doctors feared that she might even lose her sight.

That day Kate Smith told about how she prayed and how a calm faith came into her life.

When the bandages were removed, not even a blemish remained on her face. She told about that that day. Then, without any apology, she asked her radio audience to pray for Ted Collins. Later she said she believed Ted's complete recovery was due to those who prayed.

If you study the teachings of Jesus, you will find that He gave several techniques for effective prayer. The word *technique* means simply an effective way of doing something.

One tremendously effective technique that I have used through the years is this one: ". . . If two of you shall agree on earth as touching any thing that they shall ask, it shall be done for them of my Father which is in heaven" (Matthew 18:19). Suppose you have a problem or a need or a desire or an ambition. You can pray by yourself, but you are most fortunate if you can share it with some person you feel close to. It is a wonderful experience for the two of you to talk together and agree on your prayer. Some of the happiest moments of my life have been talking to close friends about how we might pray. Sometimes we disagree or we do not see it in the same way, but we keep talking and work our way through to complete agreement. Then we both pray, and I feel it is very effective. I do not explain how this idea of two people praying together gets better results than just one person alone, but I do know that many times in my own life it has been a great blessing to me to pray with a prayer partner. If you do not have one or more prayer partners, you are missing one of the most effective prayer techniques.

Praying All Night

In reference to prayer, now let me go from one extreme to the other. I mentioned the importance of praying two minutes a day. However we read this statement about Jesus: "And it came to pass in those days, that he [Jesus] went out into a mountain to pray, and continued all night in prayer to God" (Luke 6:12). Once as I read that story it hit me that never in my life had I prayed all night. I felt an inspiration to do that, and I made plans to pray all New Year's Eve night. I would begin the new year with a full night of prayer. Then the idea came to me that perhaps there were others who would like to pray with me. I was living in Atlanta, Georgia, at that time, and I phoned my friends at WSB television station and asked them when they normally went off the air. This was some years ago, and at that time they went off the air at 12:00 A.M. Then I asked when they normally came back on the air, and they said 6:30 A.M. I asked if they would be willing to let me have the TV facilities for six and a half hours, from 12:00 A.M. to 6:30 A.M., and they very graciously gave me that opportunity. At 6:00 P.M. I went to my study, and there I continued in prayer and meditation until 11:00 P.M., when I started my car and drove to the television station. At 12:00 A.M. I talked to the people about what my plans were and asked them to pray with me. I asked them to phone me with their prayer requests. Really, I was completely unprepared for what happened that night. The phone calls overwhelmed us; there was never one moment that somebody wasn't calling me. All night people poured out their prayer needs, and we prayed together.

I particularly remember one phone call, from a little girl who told me she was ten years old. She said that her parents had gone to a New Year's Eve party and had left her alone. She had heard some noises outside and was frightened, and she wondered if I would pray for her. Without thinking, I asked her the address of her home. She gave me the address, and I said over the television that if someone lived nearby to go and comfort that little girl. Later a neighbor told me that fifty-four cars came to that little girl's house that night. Of course that was too many, and if I had it to do over again, I would do it differently. But it demonstrated that when we ask, we do get answers.

In preparation for my night, I thought about how it was with the Lord the day before He prayed all night long. He probably had been very busy. He needed time to think, to be quiet, to be alone. He went out into the mountains and sat under a tree and watched the sun slip out of sight. I have seen many places in Israel where I felt He might have gone that night. I suspect He went up on a hill overlooking the beautiful Sea of Galilee. As He sat there in the quiet alone, talking with God, one by one He could see the stars, with their twinkling lights, break through the darkness. He might have thought that, just as a mother leaves a light burning for her son who is out late, the stars are God's light saying to His Son that while the Son is on earth and not in the Father's House, the Father is keeping the lights of heaven burning.

As He sat there perhaps He remembered the words of the Psalmist, "He will not suffer thy foot to be moved: he that keepeth thee will not slumber. Behold, he that keepeth Israel shall neither slumber nor sleep" (Psalms 121:3, 4). As Jesus sat out there He knew that He really was not alone. As He felt God's presence, He became rested both in soul and body. I suspect He wasn't sleepy or tired, but sustained. He felt refreshed and comforted. I know that first night when I prayed all night it never occurred to me to get sleepy.

Being there all night and not feeling any hurry, Jesus didn't feel the need to do all the talking. Suddenly, He expressed His feelings to God, and then He would be quiet. I am sure that there were times when He felt a two-way communication.

When you are in the presence of one you love and enjoy, time never hangs heavy. Soon the darkness began to lighten up, and across the horizon Jesus watched the sun begin to spread its light and warmth over the world. Surely He felt new light and warmth in His own heart and soul.

We repeated the prayer vigil other nights, and some marvelous and wonderful things happened. Many people said they wanted to spend that night entirely alone, and certainly I could understand that. On the other hand, others wanted to spend it in the company of friends. Many neighborhood parties consisted of groups who got together for the entire night. One mother wrote me when she heard of my plans, "I am inviting six of my daughter's girl friends for an all-night prayer party here in my home that night." Many churches in the city announced that their sanctuaries would be open all night that night, and people could come to pray for as long as they wished. Later many couples wrote to me and told beautiful stories of improved communication between themselves as they sat together that night.

As a theme of my first all-night prayer meeting, I used Saint Paul's words: "Brethren, I count not myself to have apprehended: but this one thing I do, forgetting those things which are behind, and reaching forth unto those things which are before, I press toward the mark for the prize of the high calling of God in Christ Jesus" (Philippians 3:13, 14).

All night long I kept lifting up four main points that Saint Paul expressed:

1. "I count not myself to have apprehended." He was not content with his life. He wanted to live higher, to be more. Too many people go through life merely existing, missing the boundlessness of real living. New Year's Eve is a time to set some new goals, to make new resolutions. As I prayed all night I kept thanking God for His blessings and my accomplishments, but I also kept re-

minding myself that I could do so much better; there was so much more in life than I had achieved, and I wanted God to put into my mind and heart higher and holier and more unselfish ambitions.

I kept a pad and a pencil there on the table before me, and as ideas came for improvement and growth in my own life I would jot them down. Before the night was over I had some marvelous goals.

2. "This one thing I do." Looking at the pad upon which I had written new goals, I could see I had written more than I could ever hope to undertake in one year. Little by little I began to set my priorities. A major goal I had that night was to decide on the one most important thing I could undertake in my life the coming year. I talked to people about it. Later I got a lot of mail from others who had followed my direction. Some had decided on a particular habit they wanted to overcome; others wrote in reference to guidance in a very special decision; some said they were praying for strength to meet a particular need; many wrote of a prayer for a special person. There is great power when we become definite and specific in our prayers.

3. "Forgetting those things which are behind." Certainly in prayer there come times to settle some things. The last night of an old year reminds us that we are leaving that year, and let's not carry some things with us into the next year. Each of us has made mistakes. We feel shame and regret, but we thank God for forgiveness! These words are so meaningful to me: "If we confess our sins, he is faithful and just to forgive us our sins, and to cleanse us from all unrighteousness" (1 John 1:9). As we pray and as we confess, we have the promise of forgiveness. Forgiveness does not blot the sin out of our memories, but it does blot it out of God's memory. I love those words of the Psalmist, "Blessed is he whose transgression is forgiven, whose sin is covered" (Psalms 32:1).

As we pray it is also a time to forget grudges, hurts, hard feelings, and wrong attitudes. In my many years of counseling, I have found that the inability to forgive someone else probably causes more harm than anything else.

4. "Reaching forth unto those things which are before." As we pray there comes a moment when we need to take that first step. Great inspiration and marvelous new insights come to one through prayer. Prayer is quietness and meditation, but prayer is also an action. Prayer that does not include action is not real prayer.

I have always felt that one of the greatest inspirations of New Year's was to make resolutions. I know some people say flippantly, "I quit making New Year's resolutions." But those people probably need to start again. A resolution is the beginning of action.

So—two minutes or all night—"Let us pray."

Praying for Other People

Dr. Frank C. Laubach and his book *Prayer, the Mightiest Force in the World* have been great blessings in my own life. I think the secret of Dr. Laubach's power was that he was so concerned about praying for other people. He tells a fable about heaven and hell. In hell the people sit on both sides of a table, but their arms are straight and stiff, so they cannot get the food to their mouths. In heaven they sit aound the same kind of table, with the same straight arms, but with one difference: They feed one another across the table.

That fable may not be true in reference to heaven and hell, but it is certainly true in reference to our earth right now. Our thoughts and prayers can become too self-centered. Dr. Laubach believed in a type of "human radar" or "sixth sense." He could reach out from one person to another through the power of prayer. He developed the habit of praying silently for other people and observing their reactions. Here let me list several examples which I got from him: He told of seeing a man sitting in an open window a half block away. Dr. Laubach shot a rapid-fire prayer at that man, saying three or four times a second, "Jesus, friend, Jesus is coming to you." In thirty seconds that man put his head in his hand and bent over in a posture of prayer.

Once, on a train, he was sitting behind a lady. He began to pray for her. He had never seen her before and knew nothing about her. As he prayed, suddenly she turned around and said to him, "What this world needs is more religion." He asked her why she made that comment to him, and she replied that she did not know, but she "just felt like talking about it."

When I first came to the First United Methodist Church in Houston as pastor, we began televising our services. We put on top of our church a microwave transmitter that sent our signals to the tower at the television station. But after a few years, tall buildings were erected around the church, and our transmitter became ineffective. The buildings blocked it off; between many people and God, there seems to be something blocking the signals. Imagine a triangle consisting of God and two persons; that first person can see God and see the other person and can become a means by which the signal can be transmitted from man to God and God to man. This is one of the things that praying for other people accomplishes.

Many times when we cannot do anything else, we can pray, and often prayer is the most effective thing we can do. When we think of those two minutes of prayer, or when we think about all night in prayer, we should always remember somebody else for whom we can pray. We should also develop the habit of praying for people we have never seen before; marvelous and wonderful things would happen in this world if we became a world of prayer people.

Dr. Laubach said that when he did not pray, people seemed neither interested or friendly to him. He felt that he was "personality zero." When he prayed, then the strange, sweet kindliness began to appear on people's faces, and they looked at him with both joy and concern.

More than thirty years ago, I learned another thing from Dr. Laubach. He emphasized that thinking is a process of talking to the inner self. Many people spend their time talking to themselves, but he said we could develop the practice in our thinking of talking to Christ and make it a two-way conversation. As we talk to Christ we find ourselves saying, "Lord, what art Thou saying to me?" Then we let our imaginations work while we reply what we suppose Christ is answering. Marvelous and wonderful experiences come out of such inner conversations.

Truly prayer is the mightest force in the world.

Affirmative Prayers Always Get Proper Results

Many years ago, a man in Chicago, by the name of Jack Smith, ran a health club. At one time he was a prize fighter; then he became a truck driver, and then a taxi driver. Finally he got his health club. Over his desk he put a big card with six letters of the alphabet printed on it. The letters were, APAGPR.

Naturally, such a sign attracted a lot of attention and people asked him what it meant. That gave him the chance to say, "Those letters mean 'Affirmative prayers always get proper results.' " Then he would talk to his customers about results of prayer. I would have liked to have known that man.

When I was a very young preacher, I moved to Thomson, Georgia, where I spent four of the happiest years of my life. In Thomson was an industrial plant called the Thomson Company. There they made clothes. Mr. L. D. Berry, the general manager of that plant, employed me as a part-time chaplain at what was then a fine salary. I spent one day a week in that plant, counseling.

We talked about it, and the company agreed to shut down the entire plant for thirty minutes each week and let me talk to the people about spiritual things. One day I received a letter from the president of that company, who invited my wife and me to come to New York, where their general offices were located. That was a great experience for us; we had never been to New York. We were greatly impressed with our suite at the Plaza Hotel. Hildegarde was having her program in one of the rooms downstairs, and we heard her with joy and appreciation. The company arranged wonderful sight-seeing tours for us, tickets to plays, and dinners. The day before we were to leave, we went up to the office of Mr. Johnson, the president, high up in the Woolworth Building. We stood at the window and looked out over New York City. It was a fascinating experience for a young country preacher and his wife. Then Mr. Johnson said to me, "I guess you wonder why we asked you to come to New York?" I said to him, "No, sir, I have been so fascinated by being here that I haven't had time to wonder why." Then he told me they had been so impressed with the results of having a spiritual influence in their plant that they wanted to offer me a job to work full-time with their company as a chaplain. I felt I should remain as the pastor of a church, but I was greatly impressed by the attitude of the president of a great industrial organization.

I believe that a spiritual emphasis in our great industrial plants can have a tremendous and wonderful influence. One of the greatest groups of ministers in America today is the chaplains of industry. I rejoice that they are growing both in number and in effectiveness.

Later when I moved to Atlanta, Georgia, for some years I served in a similar capacity with Southern Bell Telephone Company. One day I was in the office of Mr. Hals Dumas, the president of the company, and he talked to me at great length about how he felt my work there as the chaplain had had very noticeable and positive influence on the spirit of the people I worked with. That was one of the happy relationships of my life.

Thinking of prayer, let me suggest three positive steps:

1. We must analyze our prayers because sometimes we really are not praying at all. In *Hamlet* Shakespeare describes the king going to the church to pray, but his prayers were futile. The king did not feel that his prayers were even reaching the ceiling. After a while he gave it up and walked out of the church. In front of the church he said:

> My words fly up, my thoughts remain below;
> Words without thoughts never to heaven go.

The Psalmist said the same thing: "Let the words of my mouth, and the meditation of my heart, be acceptable in thy sight, O Lord, my strength, and my redeemer" (Psalms 19:14).

Here is one of the main reasons we get weak results from prayer. We say words we do not feel in our hearts. One Sunday during the morning service, I was standing in the pulpit, and I began to laugh. I was embarrassed at myself, but I couldn't help it. We were singing one of the most beautiful prayers in the hymnbooks:

> Take my life, and let it be
> Consecrated, Lord, to thee,

Then we got down to these words:

> Take my silver and my gold—
> Not a mite would I withhold.

I began looking at some of the people in that church. I had been trying to take some of their silver and gold for the Lord.

Suppose the Lord did right now what they are asking Him to do, I thought. Some of the people would have jumped out the window; they were singing it, but they didn't really mean it.

The same thing is true about prayer. The Lord's Prayer only has sixty-six words; you can say the Lord's Prayer in twenty seconds; but you can spend a lifetime learning to pray those sixty-six words. "Our Father": We could put a period right there and spend a long time. What does the word *our* mean? It means every person on this earth without any exception, and when we say those words then we recognize that every other person is our brother or sister. "Thy will be done in earth." It is easy to talk about all the glories of heaven, but when we start talking about applying the principles of God to our society, then it becomes different. Someone asked me not long ago, "Do you believe in the social gospel?" The person who prays the Lord's Prayer would never ask a question like that. If we do not want God's kingdom to come on earth and are only thinking of some "pie in the sky," then we miss the point altogether. "Forgive us . . . as we forgive." Think of one person who is hard for you to forgive, and then say that you want God to deal with you exactly as you deal with that person. Is that what you want?

No person can pray everything. The important thing to do is decide what you can pray and then pray.

2. Then I need to ask myself the question *Am I praying a proper prayer?* Would God be in harmony with that prayer? Would God help me to get even with somebody who had done me wrong? Would God use His power to give me unfair advantage over somebody else? Can I properly pray just to exalt myself, to inflate my own ego? If I pray for things just for the purpose of showing off, would God answer that prayer?

God is concerned about our material needs. We should always remember that God created this world in which we live. It has fertile fields and running streams, beautiful sunrises, majestic mountains. This world is a marvelous place given to us by God. He is concerned about our physical needs as much as our spiritual needs. However, when we pray, it is great to remember the words of our Lord, "But seek ye first the kingdom of God, and his righteousness; and all these things shall be added unto you" (Matthew 6:33).

3. The final important factor is the technique of visualization. Visualization means to take your prayer, check to see if it is a real prayer, check it according to the Spirit of Christ, then put it on the screen of your mind as a picture. Visualize it. See it already accomplished. See its form and structure already built. Let it be built in your mind, built in your heart, built in your prayers.

Then remember the words of Jesus, "And all things, whatsoever ye shall ask in prayer, believing, ye shall receive" (Matthew 21:22). When you see it on the screen of your mind, then the great struggle is to believe. Notice it says, "all things are possible"; it does not say *actual*. Believing makes us realize that nothing is hopeless. When we can believe, then we can be certain it is possible. We cannot believe impossibilities. Then we begin to feel "The things which are impossible with men are possible with God" (Luke 18:27). We begin to realize that possibilities can become actualities. We recognize our own inabilities, but believing, we have faith in God's power. We begin to put ourselves in God's hands, being anxious to eliminate anything in our lives that would block God out, letting His spirit flow through. Then we cease thinking how we can control God, but begin thinking how God can control us.

Affirmative prayers always get proper results.

EIGHT

Breaking Out of Those Prisons of the Spirit

In the year 1199, John became King of England. He was a tyrant, a yoke upon the people. Gradually, the people rebelled and finally organized what they called "the army of God and the Holy Church." On June 15, 1215, this "army" met John at Runnymede and forced him to sign the Magna Carta. That document has been described as the greatest and most enduring landmark of English liberty. The English recognize it as their greatest guarantee of freedom.

On July 4, 1776, a paper called the Declaration of Independence was adopted by the American Congress. This blessed document eventually made America "the land of the free." It is the very foundation of our national life.

Later there was a race of people in bondage in America. Slaves were bought and sold like cattle. They had absolutely no rights. On September 23, 1862, Abraham Lincoln read the Emancipation Proclamation, a document proclaiming liberty for a race of people.

The letter of Saint Paul to the Galatians is the Magna Carta, the Declaration of Independence, the Emancipation Proclamation of the Christian faith.

The great struggle in the early Christian church was to keep from making it a narrow sect. That struggle remains after nearly two thousand years. I get so tired of certain groups of people who call themselves Christians and think that everybody who is not exactly like them is unchristian. I love the words of John Wesley, who said, "If your heart beats with my heart in love and loyalty to Jesus Christ, then give me your hand."

Saint Paul's message to the Christians in that day and in this day, is, "Stand fast therefore in the liberty wherewith Christ hath made us free . . ." (Galatians 5:1). I think Saint Paul would have liked the words of the great poet Johann von Goethe:

> Yes! to this thought I hold with firm persistence;
> The last result of wisdom stamps it true;
> He only earns his freedom and existence
> Who daily conquers them anew.

We hear a lot about freedom these days. But there is only one real freedom. An Adolf Hitler can put a Martin Niemöller into jail, but he cannot take away his freedom. Our government can preserve our Bill of Rights, but no government can really give us freedom. The only real freedom is within our own souls. Saint Peter reminds us how Jesus "preached unto the spirits in prison" (1 Peter 3:19). He was not talking about people who were locked up in cells. He was talking about people imprisoned within their souls. Christ came to set people free, and here I would like to mention four prisons of the spirits of men and women:

1. So many lives are cramped and heavy laden by drudgery. The dawning of each new day brings no thrill; there is nothing to look forward to but the same old work. Monotony settles upon our souls. We have no vision and no purpose.

When I was a little boy, my father told a story, and I suppose every preacher who ever lived has told this same story. Three men were working at the task of laying brick. One of those men was saying, "I have to lay so many bricks a day." The second man was saying, "I am earning so many dollars per day." The third man was saying, "I am helping to build a great cathedral."

To the first two men, their work was drudgery, and they were glad when quitting time came. To the third man the work was exciting and wonderful. A high and holy purpose takes us out of the prison of drudgery. Some housewife wrote these beautiful words:

> Warm all the kitchen with Thy love
> And light it with Thy peace.
> Forgive me all my worrying.
> Make all my grumblings cease.
> Thou who didst love to give men food
> In room or by the sea
> Accept this service that I do
> I do it unto Thee.
>
> AUTHOR UNKNOWN

2. Another prison of our spirits is things. Many people rather than possessing things, are possessed by things. We can become owned by a house, clothes, car, money in the bank, and so forth. If day after day we are only working for things and have no vision beyond them, then they become our masters.

Some tribes in Africa used to catch monkeys in the trees by taking a gourd and cutting a hole through the gourd, just large enough for a monkey to put his hand into. In the gourd they put some nuts; they would tie the gourd securely in a tree. The monkey would put his hand in the gourd and take hold of the nuts, but in doubling up his fist, he could not withdraw his hand. He was not willing to turn loose the nuts; therefore he was trapped, and the natives could easily capture him. He was mastered by things.

Harold Bell Wright said:

Eyes blinded by the fog cannot see truth.
Ears deafened by the din of things cannot hear truth.
Brains bewildered by the whirl of things cannot think truth.
Hearts deadened by the weight of things cannot feel truth.
Throats choked by the dust of things cannot speak truth.

When we set our hearts on the spiritual, the prison wall of things will crumble and fall about us. In the Book of Galatians we read these wonderful words, "But the fruit of the Spirit is love, joy, peace, longsuffering, gentleness, goodness, faith, Meekness, temperance: against such there is no law" (Galatians 5:22, 23). Really and truly, aren't these what matter the most in our lives?

3. A third prison is a feeling of guilt. We feel we have done something that is wrong, and the burden presses down upon us. One of the best friends I have had across the years of my life was in this prison. He was a man of great ability and became very outstanding, but he had taken some money dishonestly in order to maintain his standard of living. He had reached the point where he could not repay the money, and rather than face the consequences, he jumped out his office window, and his body was spattered on the pavement.

Judas and Peter were both in this very prison. One ended up a suicide; the other heard the Lord saying to him, "... Simon, son of Jonas, lovest thou me? ..." (John 21:16). Simon heard, and he responded and became probably the greatest leader the Christian faith has ever had. Study the names that the Popes of the Catholic church have taken for themselves: We have had Pope Paul and

Pope John and many others, but there has never been a Pope
Peter. No pope has ever felt worthy to take the name of Peter.
Peter was loosed from his feeling of guilt and shame because he
accepted the fact that Christ still loved him, and he loved Christ.
That is the most important thing to remember.

A little boy's mother was very sick. She was in such a condition
that it was not advisable for her to try to talk. This little boy was
worried about her, and he realized that he had disobeyed her. He
wrote on his slate: "I have done something you told me not to do.
I am sorry. If it is all right, wipe the slate clean." He gave the slate
to the nurse, who took it in to the mother. Of course the slate was
brought back clean.

The main purpose to which I have dedicated my entire life is
telling people that no matter what you have done, God still loves
you, and God will wipe the slate clean, and you can start over
again. Not far from New York City there is a grave. On the stone
of that grave is just one word: *forgiven.* There is no name, no date
and no other description. That stone should speak to every one of
us. It does not matter who you are or when and where you live;
the word *forgiven* can be written over your life.

4. One other prison is the fear of death. Once I was riding with
the funeral director out to the cemetery after I had conducted a
funeral. As we were riding along in the procession, he made a
startling statement: "Do you realize that you preach every Sunday to a hundred people who will be dead before the next Sunday?" For many years I have preached on radio and television; I
have been told that in the Houston hospitals many patients listen
to me every Sunday morning. I began to realize that the last sermon or even the last word about God that many of those people
ever hear is from me during that sermon. In addition to those
people, I preach through the years to thousands and thousands of
shut-ins. They live in their homes and, not able to get out, they
only go to church through the radio or the television. They realize

that life for them has pretty much gone, and they do not have many years to look forward to on this earth.

I have found myself increasingly concerned about saying something about eternal life in every sermon. Death is not a blind alley to oblivion, but an open road to the Father's House.

When I go to the Holy Land, one of the places where I always feel especially close to the Lord is at the grave of Lazarus. While He was standing there that day, the Bible says, "Jesus wept." I used to preach a sermon on sympathy, and I used those words of Jesus as my text. I did not discard the sermon, but I did realize that was the wrong text. Why did Jesus weep at the grave of Lazarus? Did He weep because Lazarus had died, because he was separated from his friends? The answer is no. Did He weep out of sympathy for Mary and Martha, the sisters of Lazarus? No. Jesus wept because He was going to bring Lazarus back from the Father's House to this earth.

Not long ago, a mother and father were telling me how their son went away to college. They had never been separated before, and it was a very sad time when he was gone. They missed him so very much and confessed to me that at times there were tears in their eyes because of their longing to see their son. Then some financial reverses came into their lives, and they simply did not have the money to keep that boy in college. So they were compelled to contact him and tell him he would have to leave college and come back home. But the sorrow of bringing him back home was far greater than being separated in the first place. They wanted their son to have all the advantages of college.

If we really knew what eternal life is like, we would not bring one of our loved ones back, even if we could.

It is normal to want to live, but it is abnormal to live in fear of death. One thing we can be certain about is that we are going to die. Therefore why worry about it; why not live the best we can and take death when it comes? It should not be a prison.

Personality

In one form or another we are all concerned with the development of our personalities.

Personality can mean many things, but to me one of the major things it means is the impression we make on other people. Through the years, I have known people who felt that the way to impress other people was with smutty jokes, profanity, and an unclean attitude toward life. Someone expressed it this way: "The consciousness of clean living is, in and of itself, a source of moral strength, second only to that of a clean conscience."

When I was in college, every year each fraternity would elect the sweetheart of the fraternity. In my fraternity we would discuss our election at some length. There were always some girls around who thought they had to be smutty in order to be smart, but I noticed that the fraternities would elect clean and wholesome girls of whom they could be proud. I have come to the conclusion that "being clean" is probably the most powerful influence on one's personality.

Here let me quote from the Bible one of the most marvelous stories. Few people ever read the Book of 2 Kings, but let me quote the story just as it is written and ask each one reading this page to carefully consider this story:

> And Elisha sent a messenger unto him, saying, Go and wash in Jordan seven times, and thy flesh shall come again to thee, and thou shalt be clean. But Naaman was wroth, and went away, and said, Behold, I thought, He will surely come out to me, and stand, and call on the name of the Lord his God, and strike his hand over the place, and recover the leper. Are not Abana and Pharpar, rivers of Damascus, better than all the waters of Israel? may I not wash in them, and be clean? So he turned and went away in a rage. And his servants came near, and spake unto him, and said, My father, if the prophet had bid thee do some great thing, wouldest thou not have done it? how much rather then, when he saith

to thee, Wash, and be clean? Then went he down, and dipped himself seven times in Jordan, according to the saying of the man of God: and his flesh came again like unto the flesh of a little child, and he was clean.

2 Kings 5:10–14

Naaman did not want to wash in the Jordan River; he wanted to wash in the rivers of Damascus. Damascus represented earthly power at its greatest. Damascus was noted for the fine steel it produced; a sword made in Damascus was the strongest and best obtainable. Saul of Tarsus was on the road to Damascus when he saw the light in the heavens, heard the voice of the Lord speaking, and was converted and changed. The phrase, "on the road to Damascus" symbolizes a soul absorbed in material things. Saul's conversion means "turning around," and a power from heaven greater than this power he was seeking on earth was revealed to him there.

The two rivers of Damascus in which Naaman wanted to wash were named Abana and Pharpar. He thought that they were better than all the waters of Israel. Abana stands for knowledge; Pharpar represents skill or efficiency. On the other hand, Jordan represented a relationship with God.

Naaman was saying—and it sounds strangely modern—"Why bother about religion when we have such vast stores of knowledge and so many wonderful inventions of skill?" Take praying for the sick, for example. Why bother to pray for anybody who is sick, when we have the finest hospitals ever known to man; they are filled with equipment and can do almost anything. We have doctors and surgeons, hospital staffs who have marvelous scientific knowledge at their disposal. Isn't all that enough? Why do we need to bother to pray? Why bathe in Jordan when we have the rivers of Damascus?

Some time ago, I read of a poll of high-school students to determine what it took to be popular. The results went something like this:

1. You must have a sporty red car.
2. You must have a pleasing voice.
3. You must be friendly.
4. You must be considerate of others.
5. You must be well groomed.
6. All these things do not really matter, if you have a sporty red car.

I really do not think many young people believe the above, but sometimes we act that way.

Being clean not only means washing our bodies and having a clean mind, it also means to immerse ourselves in the cleansing, healing power of God's love. We need to realize that personality does not come from gadgets; it comes from God.

It isn't that we need to choose between the rivers of Damascus, representing knowledge and skill, and the rivers of Jordan, representing God; the truth is we should have them both. Some time ago I was in another city, speaking at a large banquet. On the way to the banquet, the pilot flew much of the way through thick clouds. I wondered how he would find the city; however, after a while he began to let down, and he came right into the runway at the airport. I thanked God for the scientific equipment that enabled him to accomplish that. We need the instruments that can guide a great airplane through blinding clouds. However we also need Him who can guide a life in the right path. One of my favorite hymns reminds us:

> What'er I do, where'er I be,
> Still 'tis God's hand that leadeth me.

When I arrived at the airport, a man who has a dual responsibility met me. He is a high official in one of the largest corporations in that city; also he serves on the faculty of one of its universities. When we got into his car, he told me we had plenty of time, so he would like to show me something of the city. I found it to be a most interesting place, but as we looked at the city I found myself becoming more and more intrigued by that man. I have been talking about personality: He truly had it. Somehow in his presence you feel drawn to him. I noticed that evening as we stood greeting one another before the meeting was to begin, people seemed to congregate around him. He seemed to be the center of attention. I kept studying him and kept asking myself what his secret was.

After the banquet was over, he was driving me back to my hotel. We went through the campus of the university, and he said, "I want to show you one more thing." He stopped before a lovely building that still was lighted. As we walked in he spoke in subdued tones. He explained to me this was the university chapel. He told me about the windows; he talked about the organ; he had a sense of reverence as we walked around that lovely building. I said to him, "Do you come here often?" He replied, "Oh yes, I never want to be in too big a hurry that I do not have time to come here for meditation." Here was a man who bathed both in the rivers of Damascus and in the rivers of Jordan. He was one who was cleaned with the white water, and out of that cleanliness came marvelous personality.

In His Will Is Our Peace

The great and wise Dante said this: "In his will is our peace."

I think of those words every time I kneel at the rock in the Garden of Gethsemane. There Jesus prayed, "... Nevertheless not my will, but thine, be done" (Luke 22:42). I always ask myself why that complete surrender to the will of God brings such happy peace into our lives. When I contemplate it, I think of four reasons why I find peace through the acceptance of God's will for my life:

1. It takes away the fear of getting lost in life. I was in a small two-seater airplane with a friend of mine, flying across the country. He did not have a radio in the plane to guide it. He was visually following his way. Suddenly he said to me that he was lost. There were no landmarks he recognized; the ground below was rough, and there was no place to land. There was some fear of running out of gasoline, and for me, there followed some very uncomfortable moments. Finally he saw something he recognized and got back on course, and got back to our landing field. Being lost—not knowing the way—can cause very real fear.

It is fascinating to study the migration of birds. Take, for example, the Pacific Golden Plover. Those birds are hatched in the northlands of Alaska and Siberia. Before the young ones are old enough to fly great distances, the old birds desert them and fly far away to the Hawaiian Islands. The young birds are left behind to grow strong enough to follow their parents.

One day these birds rise into the sky and set their course out over the Pacific. They have never made that journey before, and they must cross 2,000 miles of ocean with no marks to guide them. During this trip they have not even one opportunity to stop for rest or food, and frequently they encounter high winds and storms. Yet unerringly they fly straight to those tiny specks in the Pacific, the Hawaiian Islands.

How do you explain the flight of those birds? Surely God has provided for those birds something akin to our radio beams— something they can follow without getting lost. I firmly believe God has made the same provisions for mankind. When our lives are in harmony with His will, "on the beam," even though we cannot see the way ahead, we have an instinctive sense of the right direction. With courage and confidence, we move steadily ahead through life, without any fear of getting lost, knowing that through the storms and uncertainties, we shall come to the right place at last. That is a wonderful assurance to possess. "In all thy ways acknowledge him, and he shall direct thy paths" (Proverbs 3:6).

2. A second reason why "In his will is our peace" is true is that it relieves us of the burden of the responsibility for tomorrow.

If you will study your fears and worries, you will see that most of them are concerned not with the failures and mistakes of yesterday, because in most cases you can overcome those. Neither are most of your fears and worries about things of this very moment, because you know you can make it through this day. When you turn your face toward the dim unknown of tomorrow, you are not sure what lies in your path, and as you wonder often you worry and become afraid.

When God asks us to follow His will, at the same time He is saying, "I will accept the responsibility for whatever happens." After Jesus had said on the cross, ". . . It is finished . . ." He then said, "Father, into thy hands I commend my spirit" (John 19:30, Luke 23:46). It was a cry of faith. He had done His best; He had given His all. Now He was willing to leave the results in God's hands.

Because we have faith in God, we can say with the hymn writer:

> Keep thou my feet; I do not ask to see
> The distant scene—one step enough for me.

God usually does not make known His will to us for years ahead. Instead He shows us one step at a time, and as we take the step we know it leads us much closer to the very best possible life there is for each of us. What that life will turn out to be is not our responsibility; it is God's will, and thus we need have no fear.

Some have been forced to face great tragedies: It may be the untimely death of a loved one, a physical deformity, a bitter disappointment that seems impossible to correct.

But the completion and fulfillment of God's will is not limited to this life here on earth. He plans in terms of eternity, and though God may seem defeated, let us reserve our judgment until the complete story is written.

3. Another way in which God's will brings us peace is by eliminating the conflicts within our lives. Instead of squandering our energies with countless decisions, wondering whether to do this or to do that, we can settle it with one great decision: "I shall do the will of God." This attitude brings into our lives a singleness of purpose that provides peace and strength. We remember how Saint Paul said, "This one thing I do." When we reach that point, most problems of life are solved. Accepting the will of God gives to us the power of a great purpose.

Self-dedication to the will of God eliminates the conflict between right and wrong. A man was in to see me sometime ago about a wrong in his life. He wanted to do right, but he also wanted to do wrong, and in the resulting conflict he had become miserably unhappy. Truly, "In his will is our peace."

4. "In his will is our peace" is true for another reason, because when we follow God's will, we have the approval of a good conscience.

I know that conscience is something hard to explain, and whatever it is, it must be trained and developed. Some people have done very evil things, yet they were following what they thought were the dictates of their consciences. But after the psychologists have said all they can in explaining the human conscience—and some of them even explain it completely away—still we recognize a voice within saying, "This is right; that is wrong."

We argue with ourselves and say, "Everybody else is doing it." If we feel we have done wrong, we cannot be completely at peace until we have made it right. Huckleberry Finn was right when he said, "Conscience takes up more room than all the rest of a fellow's insides." When we do what God wants us to do, it makes us feel mighty good inside.

I now cherish many of the stories my father told me of his own life. One I have thought about a great deal is one I think bothered him all his life. I remember sadness in his voice as he told it. When he was a boy, living up in the north Georgia mountains of White County, life was simple, and they did not have many things.

As a boy he especially wanted a Barlow knife more than anything else. One day his father was going to Gainesville, and he told him to clean off a certain creek bank while he was away. For doing that job, he would bring him the Barlow knife he so badly wanted.

Eagerly my father set out to do the work in happy anticipation of his father's return and the receiving of his blessed reward. When he got down to the creek, the weather was hot, and the water was so inviting he decided to take a short swim. Playing in the water, the time swiftly passed, but then, there was no special hurry. It took a long time for a wagon to go from Loudsville to Gainesville and back. He could easily get the work finished tomorrow. The next day as he started his work he happened to see some little fish jumping in the creek. It would do no harm to catch a few, so he dug some bait, and the fish were biting. Again the hours sped by until the chance to get his job done was gone.

That night his father would be coming home. Faithful to his promise, he would have that prized Barlow knife. But that boy was now very unhappy. He would have to face his father and say, "I didn't do the job. I didn't earn the knife."

It is easy to think of our Lord. He had many temptations to turn aside, to waste His time and His life. In faithfully following

His Father's will sometimes the going was hard. But one day, the Bible says, He "lifted up his eyes to heaven, and said, . . . I have finished the work which thou gavest me to do" (John 17:1, 4). As He hung on the cross, again He said, ". . . It is finished . . ." (John 19:30).

God has given us certain tasks in life. And I know of no greater happiness we can experience than to know we can face God saying, "I've done my best."

Are You a Timid Soul?

Are you a timid soul? Timidity is one of the stumbling blocks in the paths of a lot of people.

Mr. H. T. Webster for many years drew a very popular cartoon about a character named Caspar Milquetoast. He was a sad, unhappy, weak character, personifying someone with an inferiority complex. Someone asked Mr. Webster how he started drawing that cartoon, and he replied, "There is so much of Caspar Milquetoast in me that I just thought I would draw his picture. I can also say that I enjoy reading my own cartoons, for so often I see myself in them." I have a feeling that multitudes of people have seen themselves in a Caspar Milquetoast cartoon.

Someone asked Mr. Webster why he did not occasionally let Caspar assert his manhood. He replied, "If I did that, I would lose my character. I devised a method by which he can assert his manhood, a method by which he can overcome his timidity. I let him assert his boldness in his dreams."

If we could see the cherished dreams of other people, I daresay we would be surprised at the courageous and bold action they showed. This is one reason we make heroes. We see in our heroes the persons we would like to be.

Maybe the basis of timidity is that we take ourselves too seriously. I know being who I am and what I am is about the most serious thing in life, but is it really? To have ourselves on our hands and not to know what to do with ourselves gets us into all kinds of problems. We rush out to the bookstores and buy all those self-help books. Many times just reading that sort of thing makes us think of ourselves more, and we become even more frustrated.

Many years ago, I read a book entitled *How to Be a Great Preacher.* It took me two or three years to get over that book. The only way I could become any kind of preacher was just to get up and be myself and do my best.

Some time ago, I read about an organization called the Society for the Timid Souls. They had regular meetings and provided opportunities for each member of the society to perform before the group: They might stand on a stage and sing, make a speech, play the piano, or do something else. While they were performing, the audience would talk, cough, scrape their chairs, and make rude remarks. The idea was to get the performers to reach a place where such things would not bother them, and that was supposed to overcome their timidity. I never tried that method, but I do not think it would work.

I have spent my adult life as a public speaker. I have come to realize that when I give more attention to what I am trying to say and less attention to what impression I might be making, I am much calmer and more relaxed. Timidity is born out of self-centeredness.

A dear friend of mine had real problems. He was advised that he was not expressing himself forcibly enough. He was told to go out into the woods, pick out a tree, and imagine it to be a person. Then he was to use all the profanity and harsh words he could think of in that face-to-face encounter. Expressing himself in that way would be helpful, he was told. He was told that his moral code was too strict, that he should relax, that he had been an old-fashioned prude and should start doing some things he had felt were wrong. So he let down his standards considerably. It's a long story, but that man ended committing suicide.

Far better to turn to the wisest Book that has ever been written. Consider instead these words of Jesus:

> Therefore I say unto you, Take no thought for your life, what ye shall eat, or what ye shall drink; nor yet for your body, what ye shall put on. Is not the life more than meat, and the body than raiment? Behold the fowls of the air: for they sow not, neither do they reap, nor gather into barns, yet your heavenly Father feedeth them. Are ye not much better than they? . . . And why take ye thought for raiment? Consider the lilies of the field, how they grow; they toil not, neither do they spin: And yet I say unto you, That even Solomon in all his glory was not arrayed like one of these. Wherefore, if God so clothe the grass of the field, which today is, and to morrow is cast into the oven, shall he not much more clothe you, O ye of little faith?
>
> Matthew 6:25, 26, 28, 30

The great eternal God of this universe is concerned about one little bird or one little wild flower; God is also concerned far more about one of His children.

Self-reverence and egotism never really get us anywhere. We go somewhere when we get something bigger and stronger than we are.

How Can I Be Born Again?

"How can I be born again?" That was the question that was asked me, a question that has been on the lips of countless people. We know Jesus said, ". . . Ye must be born again" (John 3:7). We have heard preachers talk about born-again people. However this has caused confusion in the minds of many people.

No one can really explain the "new birth." There are other terms that are used synonymously, such as, "the Christian experience," "being saved," and many others. The important thing to remember is that this most important experience in life comes in different ways. Some people tend to feel that everybody must have the identical experience. There are those who feel disturbed because they have not had the experience they hear someone tell about. Here let us look at three very common types of new-birth experiences in the Bible.

First turn to the ninth chapter of the Book of Acts. There we read the story of the most dramatic, climactic Christian experience we can find. Saul of Tarsus was on the road to Damascus. Suddenly, he saw a light from heaven shining all around him. "He fell to the earth, and heard a voice saying unto him, Saul, Saul, why persecutest thou me?" (verse 4). He responded to that call and became a Christian, and in becoming a Christian, his name was changed from Saul to Paul.

As long as he lived, Paul could say, "A certain day at a certain place, I became a Christian."

There is a little song that goes like this:

> I can tell you now the time,
> I can take you to the place:
> Where the Lord saved me,
> By His wonderful grace.

Many people can sing that song. It might have happened in a particular church service or in one of many other places, but they know the exact moment and the circumstance. It was a dramatic, overwhelming, glorious experience. However that is not the only type of new birth. In fact, many of us do not believe it is the best type.

As an old man in prison, Saint Paul is writing to Timothy, his dearly beloved friend. Probably Paul loved Timothy more than he loved any other person on the earth at that time, and he expected Timothy to carry on his work. He wrote to Timothy,

"From a child thou hast known the holy scriptures, which are able to make thee wise unto salvation ..." (2 Timothy 3:15). He writes to Timothy, "When I call to remembrance the unfeigned faith that is in thee, which dwelt first in thy grandmother Lois, and thy mother Eunice; and I am persuaded that in thee also" (2 Timothy 1:5). He is saying to Timothy that his grandmother was a Christian and his mother was a Christian and that he grew up believing himself to be a Christian and never knowing himself to be anything else.

There has been a great change in the methods of many of our churches. In the churches in which I grew up, not much attention was paid to the children and the young people. In the summer they would have a revival. Every effort was made to stir up the emotions and high pressure people to "walk down the aisle" and express their faith. Today churches give a lot more attention to children. They are trained and nurtured before they can walk, and they are taught the Bible and the fact that God loves them, and they grow up believing themselves to be Christians and never knowing themselves to be anything else.

Many of us were prayed for before we were born. The first song we ever learned to sing was, "Jesus loves me! this I know." Before we can remember, we were taught each night to kneel at our bedsides and pray, "Now I lay me down to sleep. . . ." When we went to the table for a meal, it was the normal and natural thing to bow our heads and have a prayer thanking God for His goodness. We grew up in Christian homes. We never hated God; we never went with the Prodigal Son to the "far country."

We do know Jesus said we must be born again, but we also know that new birth can come so normally and so naturally that we never know the exact moment that it came. We cannot name a certain time and place, yet we are just as certain that it has happened to us.

For the third story, begin reading the nineteenth chapter of

Saint Luke's Gospel. Jesus came to the city of Jericho. Living there was a man by the name of Zacchaeus. Zacchaeus was both prominent and wealthy in that city, but he was also small in body. He wanted to see Jesus, but so many people lined the road that he could not see over them. So Zacchaeus climbed up into a sycamore tree to see Jesus as He went by. Then we read, "And when Jesus came to the place, he looked up, and saw him, and said unto him, Zacchaeus, make haste, and come down; for to day I must abide at thy house. And he made haste, and came down, and received him joyfully" (Luke 19:5, 6).

We see them going to Zacchaeus' home together. The curtain comes down, and you do not see them for a time, maybe two or three hours. Then the curtain comes up and you hear Jesus say, "This day is salvation come to this house . . ." (Luke 19:9). Jesus is saying to Zacchaeus that he has been saved—that he has had a Christian experience—that he has been born again.

Let us ask ourselves what happened. My answer would be that they sat quietly together in the home of Zacchaeus. Zacchaeus talked with Jesus, and as they talked he saw that the life of Jesus was so much better than his life that no matter what it cost him, he would pay the price and make a commitment to Christ. I do not think he shouted about it; I doubt if he even cried. I imagine it was just a quiet, simple decision that took place there in that room.

Many people have had quiet births in Christ, in many different places, and that experience is just as real.

The important thing is not the how but the fact of the new birth, which may take place in many different ways. When one receives the new birth, there are four important things that happen:

1. A liberating sense of forgiveness comes into one's soul. It means not so much that our sins have been taken away, but that a

relationship with God has been consummated. There comes a feeling, as the song says, "Nothing between my soul and the Savior." We feel free.

2. In the new-birth experience, there comes a new sense of power. We feel power over temptation; we feel the power to do what we formerly thought was impossible. We especially realize that God has power in His world. The last words of the Lord's Prayer take on new meaning to us: "For thine is the kingdom, and the power, and the glory, for ever. Amen" (Matthew 6:13).

3. When the Spirit of God has come into our hearts, we feel a sense of peace. It brings to us quiet hearts born of clear consciences and a sense of adequacy. No verse in the Bible describes this feeling better than these words: "Peace I leave with you, my peace I give unto you: not as the world giveth, give I unto you. Let not your heart be troubled, neither let it be afraid" (John 14:27).

4. Out of the experience of Christ in our hearts there comes an outgoing love for other people. When we are born we naturally love our mother and our father. We come to love our brothers and sisters and our families, and we come to love our friends. But when Christ comes into our hearts, then we come to love everybody.

"... Ye must be born again."

NINE
Fret Not Thyself

The first words of the Thirty-seventh Psalm are these: "Fret not thyself. . . ." We tend to blame our troubles and our worries on the circumstances of life, on what someone else has done to us. The truth of the matter is, most of our inner unhappiness results from our fretting ourselves.

There is nothing sweeter on this earth than a little baby. However sometimes a pin sticks the little baby, or it becomes thirsty or hungry or cold or uncomfortable. Then the baby does not face life in a gallant fashion; instead the baby begins to howl and scream to the top of its voice. What happens when a baby cries? It simply acts like a baby.

The Psalmist's words "Fret not thyself," say that when a pin sticks, or when we are uncomfortable, or when we are hurting, let's not act like babies. Babies never do anything to help themselves. Real grown-up people do not spend their energies in whining, in fussing, and in worrying. They seek to discover the trouble and do what is necessary to remedy it. Why do we fret ourselves? Why do we worry? Here let me give six reasons:

1. When we are tired and worn out physically, it is much easier to feel uncomfortable and unhappy. So in every life there must be

some sort of restful change. Once a preacher announced that he was going to take a vacation. One of the members of the church said, "The devil never takes a vacation." The minister replied, "That is the reason he is the devil."

Every person needs to discover some form of recreation that leads to re-creation. One can play golf, fish, read, watch television, travel—there are many things to do, but there are times when we need to get our minds off of ourselves and our daily living.

2. We fret ourselves because something hurts us.

I know a football coach who says to his players at the beginning of the season, "If you expect to play football, you must expect sometime to get hit and to get hurt." The same thing is true of life. If we expect to live, it is a certainty that somewhere along the way of life we are going to get hurt. There are three main ways that people get hurt. Sometimes we are hurt because of a severe loss. We feel the pinch of poverty, the loss of health, our ambitions are thwarted, a friendship is broken—there are many ways to lose in life.

Sometimes we are hurt because of what life withholds. Struggle as we may, often the best prizes elude us. Our finest dreams fail to come true. Many years ago, there was a popular song by Jack Yellen that reflected this:

> I'm waiting for ships that never come in
> Watching and waiting in vain
> It seems that life's stormy sea holds nothing for me
> But broken dreams and shattered schemes,
> With each day of sorrow I love to pretend
> One more tomorrow and waiting will end
> I'm waiting for ships that never come in
> I wonder where they can be.

Hope is a wonderful thing, but continued unrealized hope has the power to break our hearts. There are those who feel near to the sunset of life, yet they see themselves no nearer to the castle of their dreams than when they started. That hurts.

Finally sometimes we are bothered by what happens to other people. We suffer because a loved one suffers. More often we are jealous of the success of others. We become envious.

3. We worry because we refuse to accept life as it is. Some things in life are fixed, cannot be changed or escaped. Instead of accepting them bravely and courageously, we whine and we fret and we rebel. People often complain about the weather. There is not much any of us can do about it. Someone has written these words:

> After all, man is nothing but a fool,
> When it's hot, he wants it cool.
> When it's cool, he wants it hot;
> He always wants it the way it's not.
> SOURCE UNKNOWN

We need to remember that there are some things that we cannot change, but we must accept and make the best of.

Failure and success both exist in life, and sooner or later we expect to get a taste of both of them. A blessed, happy person does his or her best and leaves the rest and does not worry. We all have limitations. Every so often, we hear somebody say, "I can do anything anybody else can do." That is both a stupid and an untrue statement. No person can do everything that everybody else can do. God did not put all the stars in any one person's sky. God did not plant all the flowers in any one person's garden, but God gave to every person some stars and some flowers, and we find happiness in life out of what we have.

4. We become upset when we are too self-centered. Jesus never worried about anything. It is almost a sacrilege to ever think of Him fretting or fussing or worrying, because His mind and heart was set on something greater than His own life.

Once a soldier said to another soldier, "You are wounded, buddy." "Well, I'll declare," the other soldier answered. "I had not even noticed." When soldiers are in a fight, putting everything they have into it, they become lifted out of themselves, and they fail to notice their own wounds. When we become less *self-*centered and become more *cause* centered, then our worries disappear.

5. Fear strikes us down when we are at war with our own consciences. Life can become divided. We face decisions we dare not make. We hear calls we dare not answer. We see paths of duty we dare not follow. Tremendous power lies in decision.

I have spent many nights in a beautiful hotel on the Mount of Olives in Israel. Down below is the Garden of Gethsemane. Many times I get up early before breakfast and walk down that hill to that garden. I look at those olive trees where the disciples slept, and inside that beautiful church is that rock where Jesus might have prayed. It was not easy for Him. The Bible says, ". . . His sweat was as it were great drops of blood falling down to the ground" (Luke 22:44). But during that period He made His decision, ". . . Nevertheless not my will, but thine, be done" (Luke 22:42).

There is tremendous power in decisions, and some worried, unhappy, fretful people cannot make up their minds. There comes a time when we must say, "This one thing I do."

6. The supreme cause of self-fretting and worry is lack of faith in God. Let us turn back to the Thirty-seventh Psalm, which begins, "Fret not thyself. . . ." Consider this list of phrases from that Psalm:

Trust in the Lord (verse 3)
Delight thyself also in the Lord (verse 4)
Commit thy way unto the Lord (verse 5)
Those that wait upon the Lord, they shall inherit the earth (verse 9)

The Lord upholdeth the righteous (verse 17)

I have been young, and now am old; yet have I not seen the righteous forsaken, nor his seed begging bread (verse 25)

Behold the upright: for the end of that man is peace (verse 37)

And the Lord shall help them, and deliver them ... from the wicked, and save them, because they trust in him (verse 40)

The Psalmist is saying, "If you will trust in God, you do not have anything to worry about." Vital faith and worry are incompatible.

Any time a person develops an attitude of hopelessness about a situation, that person is in error. No situation is entirely desperate. In a difficult moment many people have been inspired by the words of the Psalmist, "Commit thy way unto the Lord; trust also in him; and he shall bring it to pass" (Psalms 37:5).

We cannot believe there is any situation in life God cannot handle, and when we come to those difficult moments, comfort and power come from trusting in God's ability. Jesus said, "The things which are impossible with men are possible with God" (Luke 18:27).

Think disaster and failure and you are certain to experience them. Think God and you will begin to think victory, and you are certain to experience that. Think hopelessly and you make yourself hopeless.

As we go through life we are certain to face unsatisfactory situations. Recently in my mail there were five letters from people in unhappy situations:

One was from a wife whose husband is almost insanely jealous. They have four children and no peace and harmony in their family today.

Another letter was from a schoolteacher. She wrote that she could hardly bear the thought of facing a room full of adolescents another day. She is tired of teaching, but cannot find anything else to do.

A wife wrote that her husband is good and kind until he starts drinking.

A mother wrote about her son who is planning to marry, and she feels the woman is a very unfortunate choice and will wreck his life.

The fifth one comes from an eighteen-year-old girl who wrote that her marriage to a young man was a very sad mistake. Now he has left her, but she must care for their baby. She cannot support the two of them and does not know what to do.

Day by day, for many years, I have dealt with people's problems. I say to them that they can complain and protest; they can ask why they are called upon to face such bad situations; they can claim that God is not fair and just; they can feel mistreated and become bitter and brood over it—but I tell them that those attitudes not only do not do any good; they make the situation worse, and they make themselves worse.

People can give up, lose their bounce, forget their dreams, and slump down. They can become drab and miserable and utterly fail. On the other hand, there are some better ways to face the troubles of life. Here let me suggest three things that I often say to people with problems:

First, we need to be honest with ourselves. A good question to begin with is, "Is it the situation that is hopeless, or is it me?"

I often think of the story of the man who lived in a rural area and was moving into another such area some distance away. He had never been to his new home. As he entered the community he stopped to talk to the first man there that he saw. He asked what kind of people lived there.

The townsman made an astute reply. He first asked the newcomer what kind of people lived in the community where he had been living. The answer was that they were bad, fussing, narrow people. In fact the reason he was moving was that he could not stand those people any longer.

The reply he received was, "Well, you will find the same kind of people here."

The point is, it isn't the people, it's our attitudes toward them.

In a hopeless situation begin by looking into a mirror. There is much truth in the song:

> It's not my brother, not my sister,
> But it's me, Oh Lord,
> Standing in the need of prayer.

I know our difficult life situations are not entirely our fault, and many of them may not be any of our fault. However the correction of the situation begins with each of us. We start with ourselves, and we develop a hopeful outlook.

Second, we need to take an objective attitude toward the situation. It is good to say to ourselves, "Here is the situation, what are the facts in the case?" As we begin to examine the situation from every angle, take it apart, lay it out on the table before us, we begin to understand not only the problem but some of the answers. Over and over, when I have talked with people, I have begun with the question, "Tell me what your situation is." Most of the time, after the person has carefully explained the situation, sometimes with me asking prodding questions, he or she generally knows the answer.

Once a hurricane was sweeping toward the coast of the United States. The Army Air Corps sent out a plane to meet the hurricane and investigate it. They did not fly around the hurricane or under or over it; they flew straight into the center of the hurricane, and there in the center what did they find? Not wind or rain, not storm or tumult. They found sunshine, peace, and calm.

When we can get to the very center of our own problems, somehow we lose our fear and our sense of hopelessness and feel a calmness and a power.

Third, after we look at ourselves and our problems, we begin to realize that we are not alone. Those words of the Psalmist, "Commit thy way unto the Lord; trust also in him; and he shall bring it to pass" (Psalms 37:5) come to have real meaning. We begin to know—actually know—that the things that are impossible with us are possible with God.

Feeling ourselves in the presence of God, we begin to feel a quietness. We begin to trust, we feel there is hope. I have frequently said that the most important medicine any physician has is the faith of the patient in the physician. As the patient is in the presence of the physician, before anything is done, he begins to feel a quietness and a confidence. Much more so is this true with God.

Since I can remember there is not a story in the Bible that has excited me more than the story of David killing the giant. Here was a young shepherd boy. All he had was a sling and some stones. He was going to meet a giant of whom all the enemy soldiers were afraid. David was not afraid. Every so often I turn to the seventeenth chapter of 1 Samuel and read this thrilling story. I read how the giant "disdained" the young boy; he even cursed and promised that he would kill him and feed his body to the fowls of the air and to the beasts of the field. Then David made one of the greatest statements recorded in all literature. He said to that giant, "Thou comest to me with a sword, and with a spear, and with a shield: but I come to thee in the name of the Lord of hosts . . ." (1 Samuel 17:45). Of course, we all know that David killed the giant.

So it is as we face the giants in our own lives—the hurts, the disappointments, the losses, and all the others—somehow we know that as we face life situations in the name of God, we are going to be victorious. *Hopelessness* is not a word for godly people to use. One of life's important principles is that we should never hold back our best in any situation. We should never be willing to be holdouts in life.

The most valuable lesson I ever received as a preacher came from my father, who had been a preacher for many years and was very wise and wonderful. During the first summer that I began preaching, I was telling him of my difficulty in getting enough material for my sermons. During the conversation, I described a particularly good illustration that I had recently read.

He said, "Why don't you use that illustration in your sermon next Sunday?"

I replied that I was saving that particular story for a special occasion.

My father told me, "Son, the next sermon that you preach is the most important sermon of your life. Put the very best you have into it."

Throughout my ministry I have practiced that principle. I have never used a filing system. If I have something I think is worth using in a sermon, I put in the next one I preach.

Saving is a virtue that can very easily become a fault. Some time ago I was preaching in another city. A very lovely lady more than seventy years old invited the pastor of the church and me for lunch. After lunch she began showing us some of the loveliest things she had. She opened several drawers filled with exquisite linens. There were lovely tablecloths and napkins; she showed us some of the loveliest china I have ever seen. She owned several shelves full of exquisite crystal.

I asked the lady when she used all those beautiful things, and very sadly she replied that she had never used them. She accumulated these things so carefully, but she and her husband and

her own children never used them. Now he had died, the children
were gone, and she was alone. There were tears in her eyes as she
said to us, "I saved my beautiful things too long."

We do that with ourselves. A rare person gives his or her very
best to the day's work. We keep thinking that some tomorrow we
will really give our best selves. But somehow that tomorrow never
comes. We have dreams that we allow to remain dreams; we are
not ready to begin turning those dreams into actions.

We even do this with our very lives. We save ourselves to
death.

No one of us is successful all the time, but we keep going.
Many years ago a baseball pitcher by the name of Tommy
Henrich said, "I do not believe in defeat." He went on to explain
that at the end of a game, when his team had come out on the
short end of a score, he put it out of his mind and began to get
ready for the next game. He said, "If you think victory, in terms
of God's will, you will create around you an atmosphere of
success."

E. Stanley Jones, the great missionary and preacher, described
a meeting where people were giving their own testimony. One
man stood up and said, "For me life means victory—victory—victory."

Another man got up and said, "For me life means victory
—defeat—victory."

Then a third man stood up and said, "For me life means defeat—victory—defeat." I suspect that most of us can relate to that
third man.

Some time ago I was visiting with one of the greatest ministers
in the world. I had preached that night in his city, and he had at-
tended the service. After the service, he suggested that we go out
and eat some ice cream together. That was a wonderful experience for me. We sat and talked for at least two hours. I especially
remember one thing he said: "Most of us are pagans with Christian intervals or Christians with pagan intervals."

He meant that even the worst people have moments of high victory, and even the best people have moments of humiliating defeats. However the ones who rise to the highest are the ones who think of their victories instead of their defeats.

Soon after Mrs. Henry Ford died, someone told about the early days when Mr. and Mrs. Henry Ford had no money at all. He had a dream of building a car, and Mrs. Ford believed in her husband through those very difficult times. Mr. Ford called her the believer, and she called him the dreamer. They lived happily together for sixty years. The one telling the story concluded with this line: "At last the believer has gone to rest with the dreamer, two who together are the epitome of the American story."

Persons who learn to dream and believe will always make the most of themselves.

Do Not Put Off Hoping

One of the wisest persons who ever lived was Solomon. He wrote the Book of Proverbs, and among many other wise things, he said this, "Hope deferred maketh the heart sick . . ." (Proverbs 13:12). One of the great principles of life is: Do not put off hoping. Many things we cannot get started today, but we can always begin to hope. In Tennyson's great poem *In Memoriam A. H. H.* we read this wonderful line: "The mighty hopes that make us men." Thomas Fuller said it this way, "Great hopes make great men."

Through the years I have studied, written, and preached about the Ten Commandments. One of those commandments states, "Thou shalt not take the name of the Lord thy God in vain; for the Lord will not hold him guiltless that taketh his name in vain" (Exodus 20:7). For many years I talked about using God's name in profanity. I feel today that profanity is stupid and silly and a mark of an ignorant person. When a person does not have the mental capacity to express thoughts adequately, that person turns to profanity. However I do not feel that commandment talks about using God's name in profanity. In my opinion, the most blasphemous word in the English language is the word *hopeless*. The Bible says, "Hope thou in God" (Psalms 42:5). Hopelessness is the denial of the presence and power of God. To say "My situation is hopeless" is to slam a door in the face of God.

We can be sure that life is filled with glad surprises for those who hope.

There come times in our lives when it seems we have no ground to stand on, when it seems that there is nothing to believe in, when it seems that everything is going against us. Then it is we need to turn to Romans 4:18 and read where Saint Paul talks about the great Abraham and says, "Who against hope believed in hope. . . ." That is, no matter what, never lose hope.

One of the most famous paintings of all time is G. F. Watts' painting entitled *Hope*. The portrait shows a woman sitting upon a globe. This woman is pitted against the world; her eyes are bandaged; she cannot see ahead of herself. In her hands is a harp. All the strings of the harp are broken save one. Those broken strings represent her shadowed expectations. Now only one string remains: the string of hope. Triumphantly she strikes that last one, and from it comes a glorious melody that floats out over her world and fills her dark night with stars. It is both a great painting and a great truth.

Some years after that picture was painted, Mr. Watts received a letter from a woman he had never seen, but he cherished that letter the remainder of his days. For this woman life had become unbearable. She was going down to the river to drown herself. As she walked along the street, she saw some people standing before a shop window. She stopped and looked through the window, and there she saw this wonderful painting. She looked at the forlorn picture of that woman with her bandaged eyes and the broken strings in her harp; then she saw the one string that was left, the string of hope. It so inspired her that she, too, strung the string of hope within her own soul. She turned back and tried again.

Here let us look again at what the Psalmist said, "Why art thou cast down, O my soul? and why art thou disquieted in me? hope thou in God: for I shall yet praise him for the help of his countenance" (Psalms 42:5). Even though we are cast down, disquieted, we still can hope, and in hoping we can start over and keep living. Eventually, we learn that God never lets us down, so I say: Trust your high hopes; they can carry you far.

When Trouble Comes

Sooner or later every person faces some kind of trouble. There are many types: illness, financial reverses, frustrations on the job, problems in marriage, some hurt that comes to one of our children, an unhappy relationship between parent and child, ambitions that are never realized, and many other troubles.

All of this came to my mind the other night when I sat down to read Saint Paul's letter to the Philippians. He wrote from a prison cell. There were so many places he wanted to be at that time. Churches needed him, opportunities for service abounded. A lesser man would have become discouraged, bitter, resentful.

A frustrated man would have sat in that prison cell, asking over and over, "Why has this happened to me?" Instead Saint Paul decided that he would do what he could, so he spent his time writing letters that have become precious possessions of mankind.

Paul counts his blessings. In the very first chapter of his letter to the Philippians, he wishes them well and says, "I thank my God upon every remembrance of you" (verse 3). Instead of complaining of his own troubles he says, ". . . The things which happened unto me have fallen out rather unto the furtherance of the gospel" (verse 12).

We have never been promised a life with no trials or skies that would always be sunny. Faith in God has never been declared an insurance policy against pain, but we do have the promise of companionship, no matter what happens. There come times when we remember with joy the words of Jesus, "... Lo, I am with you alway ..." (Matthew 28:20). Six very important truths need to be remembered in reference to our "trouble" experience:

1. When we are troubled, we must remember our need for each other. At a funeral service for a lovely mother I was deeply impressed as the four children stayed so close to their father and to each other. At this time of great sorrow there was a real need. In times of illness it means a lot to know that somebody cares. In fact, in the latter years of life, having the realization that somebody loves you is one of the most stimulating experiences of life. However there are those in pain who do not receive love. At that moment many people come to a realization of the greatest and highest truth that can be known on this earth. That truth is: *God loves you.* In those three words is summed up the meaning of the Christian faith. It is a glorious experience to realize God loves you.

2. In times of trouble and danger, we are more aware of the uncertainties of life and even of the uncertainty of life itself. To begin with, knowing that life is uncertain, we should make added effort to enjoy the good and the happy times we experience. In the second place, even though we are going through difficult times, there is always the possibility of something good happening. Through the years I have taken many trips in airplanes. Oftentimes you find yourself in a cloud, and it is always a sense of joy and relief when the plane breaks through the cloud into the bright sunshine. So it can be with the experiences of life. We are not sure when we will be in the sunshine and when we will be in the clouds, and so we are prepared for the uncertainties.

3. Times of trouble, whether they be illness or sorrow, are not times to solve our problems. In these times there is a tendency to

think of all of the difficulties and problems of life, which just makes everything worse. Wait until the storm has passed and then solve your problems. Illness throws us off balance emotionally. In times of trouble we have a tendency to lose our poise and equilibrium. Little things become big things when life is not going well. When we are hurting, it is much easier for our imaginations to get out of hand. A sleepless night can seem like an eternity. We can get to the place where we do not think with clarity, and things get out of proportion. In times of trouble do not let your mind become absorbed with all the other troubles of life.

4. All through the Bible we are promised dividends from our troubles. Trials and tribulations might be gold mines from which are taken some of life's richest prizes. Oftentimes instead of praying, "Lord, when am I going to get out of this?" it is better to pray, "Lord, what am I going to get out of this?"

Through the years, I have visited with many people when they were having serious problems. One of the statements in God's Word that I like to read in those moments is: ". . . We glory in tribulations also: knowing that tribulation worketh patience; And patience, experience; and experience, hope: And hope maketh not ashamed; because the love of God is shed abroad in our hearts by the Holy Ghost which is given unto us" (Romans 5:3–5). If our trouble is illness, oftentimes it gives us an opportunity to be quiet, to think, to more properly evaluate life, to develop sympathy for other people, to learn that the world can keep going no matter what happens. During times of trouble we gain a greater appreciation for God's gifts, such as health and happiness. We develop a realization of the higher purposes of life, and there is a tendency to lose some of our selfish independence and be more thankful for our dependence upon other people. During trouble we become aware of and thankful for the achievements of medical science.

5. Most importantly, in times of trouble and especially illness, we become sure of God. Once there was a woman who was trying to turn the light on in a telephone booth. A passerby said, "Lady,

if you will shut the door, the light will come on." Many times when troubles come and we shut the door, the light does come on.

> There is an eye that never sleeps,
> Beneath the wing of night.
> There is an ear that never shuts
> When sink the beams of light.
> There is an arm that never tires
> When human strength gives way.
> There is a love that never fails
> When earthly loves decay.
>
> GEORGE MATHESON

Ralph Waldo Emerson said that a man is a hero, not because he is braver than anyone else, but because he is braver for ten minutes longer.

6. Not all troubles turn out well, not all sick people get well, not all hurts in life are healed.

One of the greatest comedians the world has ever known was Sir Harry Lauder. When he heard the news that his son had been killed, he said:

> In a time like this there are three courses open to a man. He may give way to despair, sour upon the world, and become a grouch. He may endeavor to drown his sorrows in drink or by a life of wayward and wickedness. He may turn to God. It may be that he cannot overcome the pain but he can find the power to endure it.

Sarah Williams wrote a poem called, "The Old Astronomer." On that poem are these lines:

> Though my soul may set in darkness,
> it will rise in perfect light,
> I have loved the stars too fondly
> to be fearful of the night.

TEN
Cultivate Yourself

Through the years I have remembered a story about a girl saying to her mother, "Ma, what is personality?" She replied, "I don't know what it is, but whatever it is, you ain't got it."

That mother was wrong; everybody has personality. The impression you make on other people is really your personality. We wish to achieve to our happiest and best position in life. We need to constantly cultivate our personalities.

First we need to develop a wholesome sense of self-appreciation. One of the most contemptible persons we ever meet is the conceited person. Not many people are truly conceited, but a lot of people who give that impression really feel inferior in their hearts. No person should ever feel inferior, and one of our greatest mistakes is to *underestimate* ourselves. We are more than we think we are. We need to pray the prayer that says, "O Lord, give me a higher opinion of myself." Once Abraham Lincoln's mother said to him, "Abe—be somebody." Somehow Abraham Lincoln believed that could be accomplished, and he became about the most important "somebody" who ever lived in our land.

I wish I had the power to plant firmly and securely in the minds of every person to whom I have ever ministered the thought *You are somebody, and above all, be that somebody.*

One of the greatest thinkers and philosophers of all time was Immanuel Kant. Any student of philosophy knows that he was a man whose mind dealt with great thoughts. He summed up his philosophy of life in one sentence: "Two things fill me with ever increasing admiration and awe the longer and more earnestly I reflect upon them; the starry heavens without and the moral law within."

The heavens fill us with a sense of awe and wonder. We say with the Psalmist, "The heavens declare the glory of God ..." (Psalms 19:1). But let us keep reminding ourselves that just as sublime as the heavens is something within a human being. There is something within every individual that should fill that person's mind with admiration.

Believing the above to be true, we may begin to seriously release those winsome, lovable personalities within us. We need not wait until we have all the money and all the material things we have dreamed of and want. Houses and cars and clothes and jewelry and savings accounts are all good, but some of the most winsome personalities do not have any of those things.

Even though we did not get all the education we wanted, have not read all the books, and do not know as much as we would like to know, still we can operate with what we have learned and what we do know. Most of us know a lot more than we realize.

Maybe we do not hold the position in life that we have dreamed of holding. Someone is way up the ladder ahead of us, and seeing that person, we become dissatisfied and belittle ourselves. But it is just possible that inside that person is really not as well off as we are. Personality is not dependent upon position.

Your relationships with other people may not be perfect and may even be strained. This can happen between neighbors, between people you work with, between members of your own family.

One night two friends who had not seen each other in many years happened to meet downtown. They walked over to a little restaurant and began talking with each other, reminiscing about their lives. Before they realized it, it was three o'clock in the morning. Both knew their wives would be upset about their staying out so late. However they went on home. A few days later they met again. One said to the other, "How did you make out getting home so late the other night?" The man replied, "Fine. I just told my wife that I had met you and how we talked together, and she said she understood and that was fine." Then he said, "How did you make out?" The other man replied, "Well, when I came in at three o'clock in the morning, my wife got historical." His friend corrected him saying, "You mean she got hysterical." "No," the man insisted, "I mean historical—she brought up everything that had happened in the last thirty years."

Telling that stupid story reminds me of another one. On their twenty-fifth wedding anniversary, the husband said to his wife, "Honey, I have never deceived you, have I?" "No," she replied, "but you have tried many times."

Really what I am trying to say here is, there come times when we need to forget past mistakes and past failures and say, "I am who I am and what I am, and I am going to let my personality be the very best it can be." There is no need to wait until all the conditions get perfectly right.

I knew about a man who decided he would begin reading some good books. In order to do that he made careful preparations. He selected the most comfortable chair in the house and placed it in the room where he planned to read. He put on his slippers and his lounging robe; he fastened a bookrest to the arm of the chair to hold the book at just the right angle before his eyes. He set a special reading lamp by his side. After everything was perfectly adjusted, then he sat down in his chair and promptly went to sleep.

Many times we spend all our energies in getting everything ready to start, and then we have nothing left with which to start.

Most great things are not done in perfect conditions. O. Henry wrote most of his best books while he was in jail. Likewise Saint Paul wrote many of his greatest letters in jail; *Pilgrim's Progress* and *Don Quixote* were written in jail; Sir Walter Scott wrote his *History of the World* in jail. Most of us feel bound in some way, and if we wait until we get out of jail and are perfectly free, we never will do what we can do. You do not become a great personality by trying to get all the outside conditions perfectly right. You become great by rising above the conditions.

It is not things that are outside that make you: It is what is inside you. On April 13, 1936, Howard Thurston died. He was recognized as the greatest magician the world has ever known. For forty years he traveled all over the world, and more than 60 million people paid admission to his performances. He received enormous fees for his work. What was the secret of his success? Was it because he knew more about magic than anybody else knew? Thurston himself said many times that there were numerous magicians who knew as much about magic as he and who were as skillful as he. Dale Carnegie sought the answer to Thurston, and after traveling with him and watching him work, Carnegie said, "He has had the ability to put his personality across the footlights."

How did Howard Thurston get his personality? It was not because he was born with a silver spoon in his mouth. When he was a little boy, his father cruelly whipped him one day for driving a team of horses too fast. Blind with rage, that little boy ran out of the house, slammed the door, and ran screaming down the street. He did not turn back; instead he became a hobo riding in boxcars, begging, stealing, sleeping in barns and deserted buildings. He was arrested dozens of times, chased, cursed, kicked, thrown off trains, and even shot at. At the age of seventeen he found himself stranded in New York City, without any money and without a friend.

He started aimlessly walking the streets, and he happened to see a religious service in progress. He walked in and sat down. He had been there just a few moments when the speaker said, "There is a man in you." That one sentence caught hold of Howard Thurston. At the close of that service, with tears running down his cheeks, he walked down the aisle and knelt at the altar, and there he became a surrendered person to God. Two weeks later he began preaching on the street corners of Chinatown, and this is the man who became the most famous magician of all time. For forty wonderful years Howard Thurston believed "There is a man in me." He never forgot it. When we believe that there is something within us that is important, then our personalities reflect it.

Do Not Be an Empty House

Jesus told a story about a man inhabited by an unclean spirit. The spirit was driven out of him, but had no place to go, so after walking and walking and not finding any place to rest, the spirit returned from whence he came. He found his house empty, so he moved back in and took with him seven other spirits more wicked than himself. That story is found in Matthew 12:43–45. Sometimes we get so concerned about overcoming the bad things in our lives that we fail to think about filling our lives with good things. We want to get rid of our bad habits, get forgiveness of our sins, and blot out our unhappy memories. But if that is all we do, then we leave our lives empty and life ends up worse off than it was in the first place.

We need to realize that harmlessness is not holiness, that emptiness is not saintliness. Not being bad is not the same as being good. Many times we take great pride in the faults we do not have, in the sins we do not commit, in the harm we do not do.

One may be interested in having a flower garden. That person may select a plot of ground and carefully clean off all the grass and weeds growing there. However unless some flowers are planted, it will never be a garden.

Jesus was speaking to the people of His day who had the idea that the virtues of life consisted in the "thou shalt nots," so they made all kinds of rules and regulations forbidding people from doing things they decided were wrong. There was a day in the church in America when much of the preaching consisted of the *nots* of life. These preachers talked long and loud about "Thou shalt not dance, play cards, drink alcohol, smoke, buy anything on Sunday" and on and on.

The point is, we can decide what we feel is wrong, and even though we rid ourselves of these things, we are simply an empty house. The important thing is not what we do not do, but what we do do. Not only is there no virtue in mere emptiness, emptiness is actually a sin. In the Book of James we read, "... To him that knoweth to do good, and doeth it not, to him it is sin" (4:17). Jesus told about a fig tree that bore no fruit, and it "withered away" (Matthew 21:19). He told about a man who did not use his talent and buried it in the ground, and it was taken from him. We lose what we do not use. Jesus told about five women who provided no oil for their lamps, and the door to the wedding ceremony was shut in their faces. Jesus also told about a priest and Levite who passed by a wounded man and did nothing to help him. They were both condemned (Luke 10:31, 32). Jesus also told about a young man who had great possessions, but he was not willing to commit himself to the highest purposes in life, and in the end, "He went away sorrowful" (Matthew 19:16-22).

Some time ago I heard about a young couple who had gone to a theater. During the performance it was discovered that the theater was on fire. The young lady turned to her escort, but all she saw was his back as he was running out. After some time, the fire was put out and the danger was past. He came back, but she would not accept him as her escort any longer. She did not want to go with him again. Why? He did not set the theater on fire, he did her no harm. However in the presence of a possible need, he did nothing.

So the greatest danger facing a human life is not the wrong we do, but the right we fail to do.

For many years I have had a minister friend who is very successful as the pastor of a small church. Each month he asks the people to write down four things on a sheet of paper:

1. What do you plan to do this coming month to make you a better Christian?
2. What do you plan to do this month to make your homelife happier for all who live there?
3. What do you plan to do this month to make your church a more effective witness in the community?
4. What do you plan to do this month to make your community a better place for all the people who live there?

Instead of fussing at people, he turns their minds into constructive channels. Reading these questions, it occurs to me that if at the beginning of each month each of us wrote out several positive, constructive questions for ourselves and lived with them during the month, it could make a tremendous difference in our lives. Maybe if we changed our attitudes, we would change our lives. A man who had made a study of salesmen said to me recently that 20 percent of all the salesmen in the United States make 80 percent of the sales. He said the difference is a positive, constructive attitude.

In Greek mythology there is a story of how the sirens used to sing, and the ships would be lured over onto the rocks and the sailors destroyed. One sea captain worked out a defense. He stuffed the ears of his sailors with wax so they could not hear. However that not only kept them from not hearing the bad; it also shut out from their hearing the good.

Jason worked out a far better defense. When he prepared to

make his voyage, he did not stuff his sailors ears with wax; instead he hired the finest singer in the land. His name was Orpheus. When the ships neared the place where the sirens sang, Orpheus would strike his harp and begin to lift a song into the air. The music of Orpheus would be so much more wonderful than the songs of the sirens, the sailors were never tempted to leave their course.

Today many voices call people to ruin and destruction. We never win by trying to merely stop those voices or by stuffing our ears in the voice of life; we need to hear the highest and the best. We need to fill our minds with positive thoughts and our lives with constructive action.

Oh, the tragedy of an empty life.

How to Stay Young

I get excited every time I read these words: "But they that wait upon the Lord shall renew their strength, they shall mount up with wings as eagles; they shall run, and not be weary; and they shall walk, and not faint" (Isaiah 40:31).

Ponce de Leon was not the only one who sought for the fountain of perpetual youth. In one way or another each of us is seeking that fountain. We do not like to think about losing our strengths, being weary, and even fainting. We do not want to get old; we think of old age as calamity. I love the story of how one day, when John Quincy Adams was eighty years old, a friend greeted him on a street in Boston, "Good morning, Mr. Adams, how are you today?" Then came the youthful answer, "Mr. Adams is quite all right, thank you. Of course, the house he lives in is a bit dilapidated; its walls are tottering on their foundation; its roof is greatly in need of repair. I think he is soon going to have to move out of his old house into another not made with hands. However, Mr. Adams is quite all right. Thank you."

Some years ago I quoted Mr. Adams' remark in a sermon. The following week I received a letter from a woman who had heard what I had said. She wrote:

> The house in which I live is eighty-two years of age. Naturally it is not quite as beautiful as it was fifty years ago. One reason for this, perhaps, is that I have not kept it painted as is the custom today. But I have given a great deal of attention to the interior decoration. Then, I have a reliable tenant on the top floor.

Really old age is not a matter of the calendar as much as a matter of the mind. Here let me suggest four real signs of old age:

1. Magnifying trifles is the first one which comes to mind. The twelfth chapter of the Book of Ecclesiastes begins with the words, "Remember now thy Creator in the days of thy youth. . . ." This chapter goes on to talk about the burdens of old age and uses the expression, "the grasshopper shall be a burden" (12:5). What a vivid statement that is! The grasshopper is so small it is hard to imagine it ever becoming even noticeable on one's shoulder. However we are being told that we can reach the point where even the smallest things can become difficult. Magnifying the little loads of life is a sure sign of old age. As the saying goes, "Making mountains out of molehills."

2. A second sure sign of old age is timidity. This same chapter of Ecclesiastes tells us that when people get old, ". . . they shall be afraid of that which is high . . ." (12:5). We get to the place where the spirit of adventure is dead. Undertakings that once thrilled us now repel us.

Often I think about Caleb. He said to the people who were on the border of the Promised Land, ". . . Let us go up at once, and possess it; for we are well able to overcome it" (Numbers 13:30). The people were still too timid to go and possess the land the Lord had promised. Later we read one of the most tragic verses in the Bible: "For the Lord had said of them, They shall surely die in the wilderness. And there was not left a man of them, save Caleb the son of Jephunneh, and Joshua the son of Nun" (Numbers 26:65). He had still not lost his daring, youthful spirit. The other people died, but Caleb and his friend Joshua, even at the age of eighty-five, were still ready to go and possess the land.

At the age of eighty-five we can still dream and give ourselves to high adventure. On the other hand, when a person reaches the place in life where his or her highest purposes are comfort and security, then that person is old, no matter what the calendar says.

3. Glorifying the past at the expense of the present and the future is another sure sign of old age. When a person reaches the place where all the good days have dropped into the sunset, then that person is old. Ever since Adam reached his fifty-first birthday, there have been people who have been looking back to the good old days of fifty years ago. For those people all the good people are dead, and there is no hope in the next generation.

4. A fourth mark of old age is being opposed to change. Such old people do not have as their hero Abraham launching out into the great unknown with God. Instead their hero is Rip van Winkle, sleeping his unchanging way through life.

Many years ago there was a bill introduced in one of our state legislatures to buy an electric chair for execution. One member of the legislature waxed eloquent in his opposition to it and in favor of the old method of hanging. Finally, he reached the climax with these words, "Hanging was good enough for my papa, and it's good enough for me."

While thinking of the marks of old age, we do see some ideas about staying young. Let us consider these three ways to avoid the loss of our youth:

1. Face the fact that there is no way to stop bodily aging. Certainly, proper health care and sane and sensible living habits help our bodies to stay younger longer. However there is nothing we can do to stop the clock of life. We cannot avoid old age by tearing up the old family record, by refusing to admit our ages, or resenting the fact that we are not as young as we used to be.

In fact we ought to be very grateful that we are growing older. Suppose the process were reversed: Instead of growing older, we would be shrinking younger. If I had the privilege of getting younger instead of getting older, it would be the most horrible thing that could happen in my life. As the years shrunk up, I would lose each one of my grandchildren and then each one of my children and all the good and happy experiences I have accumulated all these years. I would not give up one year of my life.

2. If we would avoid old age, we must be interested in the life of today. Nothing is more withering and deadening than loss of interest. There are those in their twenties who are fed up. They face life without enthusiasm or joy. Maybe there is a lot of wrong in the world today, but this is our day and it belongs to us and it is the only day we have. It is exciting to think about tomorrow.

Many years ago Bishop Wright was an outstanding minister in America. Speaking in a college in the Midwest, he said, "Everything that can be invented has already been invented. We are now living in the epitome of civilization." Later the president of that college suggested to the bishop that perhaps some new things would be discovered, and rather defiantly, the bishop replied, "Name me one thing." The college president said, "I believe some day men will build a machine that will fly in the air."

Bishop Wright said, "That is the most stupid idea I have ever heard of. If God had wanted man to fly, He would have given him wings." It so happened that Bishop Wright had two sons, one named Orville and the other named Wilbur—the first two people to fly in a machine.

Many of us remember the first time we heard a radio. We saw that as a marvelous miracle. Then came television and how wonderful television is. However, it will not be long until we will be receiving television programs directly from satellites, and I am told that in a reasonable time in the future, you will be able to sit in your home and tune in to any one of 200 television programs. Ask yourself the question *What excites me most about the future?* If I were answering that question, I could write many things, but I think the one that excites me the most is the thought that some day we will be able to be in communication with human beings on some other planet. It may be that there is a civilization on another planet far more advanced than our civilization, and what a glorious thing it would be to be in contact. It really might happen. If that doesn't happen, I know that many wonderful things will happen, and I want to live as long as I can and see as many of those things as possible.

3. One real way to keep young was given us by the Prophet Isaiah, long ago. He said, "But they that wait upon the Lord shall renew their strength; they shall mount up with wings as eagles; they shall run, and not be weary; and they shall walk, and not faint" (Isaiah 40:31). For many of us that is one of the most thrilling promises in all the Bible.

Luigi Pirandello wrote a fascinating play called *Six Characters in Search of an Author.* The plot describes a company on the stage of a theater; they are interrupted by six other characters clambering to be in the play. They are in search of an author who will bring them to life in an actual presentation.

God has brought us to life and given us the chance to live in His marvelous and wonderful world. And He keeps saying to us, "I want to live in you and give you strength and help you run and keep you going."

Once a man who was going through a very difficult experience, quoted the words to me, "And they shall walk, and not faint."

And then he said, "I have reached the place I cannot walk, but I can crawl, and I want you to know I have not stopped." As long as we even keep crawling we are not old.

God Always Answers People

There was a woman whose husband loved her very much, and during her convalescence from a severe illness he carried her from room to room. On sunny days he would carry her onto the porch or out into the garden. He waited on her constantly. One day, the physician told him, "If you keep this up, she will never walk again. She likes being carried, and she will never even try to walk."

The husband saw the point, so when he went home that night he watched as she walked tremblingly and stumblingly. He even let her fall and painfully pick herself up. It would have been so easy to rush to her side and keep her from falling. That is what we want God to do. We blame Him when we fall, and we blame Him for not rushing to our sides to pick us up and take away all the pain. No one can ever imagine what it cost God to refrain from intervention as His own beloved Son was put to death. But God's holding back was not weakness. The cross of Christ became the power of God unto salvation.

We are promised, "And whatsoever ye shall ask in my name, that will I do . . ." (John 14:13). However there are three things that we must always remember in reference to that promise of our Lord:

1. God always distinguishes between what we really want and what we think we want at the moment. A little child might say, "I do not want to go to school." At the moment that may be the desire of the child, but the larger desire is to go to school. To give in to that momentary desire and to deny the larger life's desire

would be a tremendous mistake—a mistake that God never makes. Rabindranath Tagore said a wonderful thing: "Thou didst save me by the hard refusal." Every one of us comes to a place in life where we thank God for His refusal to answer some of our prayers.

2. God is concerned about all His children, and He will not answer one person's prayer if it means hurting other persons unworthily. Some time ago I finished my speaking engagements in another city earlier than I expected, and I was anxious to come home. I phoned for a plane reservation and was told that the plane was filled. However, I asked to be put on standby. I felt sure that there would be a vacant seat, especially since I was praying about it. I got to the airport and stood at the gate with my bag in hand, ready to board the plane. The plane came in and left, and I was still standing there. The point is: God could somehow have managed to put someone off that plane or keep someone from being at the airport that day to claim his or her reservation. But God would not have denied someone else that right in order to give me what I wanted.

I grew up in a home with seven children, and that is one of the greatest of life's blessings. You learn that if you insist on two pieces of pie, it might be that your brother or sister will not have one piece.

3. Finally God always responds. We need to remember that God may not always answer prayers, but He does always answer people.

"Whatsoever ye ask in my name, that will I do." Here is the full meaning of that promise: "Whatsoever ye ask, if it is what you really want and if it is in harmony with God's will and if it is fair to all others concerned, then God will show you how to cooperate with Him so that, together, the answer can be accomplished."

When I pray with the above thoughts in mind, then I can bring any need of my life to God with confidence, and I know that it will be heard, and I will be answered.

Overcome Your Timidity

Turn to Matthew 6 and read these words: ". . . Take no thought for your life . . ." (verse 25). That is, stop thinking just about yourself all the time, do not let your mind be completely filled with your daily cares and concerns.

Keep reading that chapter until you come to the words "Behold the fowls of the air . . ." (verse 26). Go out in the woods and in the fields, calmly look at the lovely birds, remember that God cares for them, and also remember that you are more important in God's sight than they are.

Keep on reading that chapter until you come to the words ". . . Consider the lilies of the field . . ." (verse 28). Look at the lovely flowers and plants growing out of the earth. See how God creates beauty, and think about how God is more interested in bringing beauty out of our own lives.

Keep on reading until you come to those words ". . . Seek ye first the kingdom of God . . ." (verse 33). That is, stop thinking about yourself and think about something you might give yourself to.

Timidity is a form of self-reverence and egotism. When we quit thinking about ourselves and start thinking about something greater, our characters become transformed. Some time ago a young lady walked into my office. She talked to me about the facts that she was an artist and wanted to open her own studio. She had spent a lot of time thinking about it; she wanted a minister to pray with her that she was doing the right thing and to ask God's guidance in her undertaking. I asked her about herself and her life, and she told me a marvelous story. She was a very shy person. As a very young child she was severely burned over a large part of her face. The burn left terrible scars and very early in life she became deeply conscious of those scars. Sometimes at school, when she was a child, she would hear other children remark behind her back about her scarred face. She went to doctors, and they improved the appearance of the scars, but could not completely eliminate them.

Later she went to art school, but she did not do as well as she wanted. It seemed that her teachers were uninterested in her. Oftentimes a teacher would walk among the students in the art class as they were painting and stop at the student next to her and offer suggestions and compliments and then frequently completely ignore her and go on to the student on the other side. She felt very disheartened and discouraged.

One day she read two statements that completely changed her life. One was the statement of Saint Paul: "I can do all things through Christ which strengtheneth me" (Philippians 4:13). The other statement was from Ralph Waldo Emerson, "Neither you nor the world knows what you can do until you have tried."

The next day she went to art school as usual, but she felt different. All day long those two sentences kept running through her mind. She told me that was the shortest day she had ever lived. She got more done that day than ever before, and at the close of the day, instead of feeling tired, she felt strong and refreshed. Usually at the close of the day she would hurry away from the art school and go home. But one afternoon she decided to take the time to wash out all her paintbrushes. While she was behind the little partition, washing her brushes, the art teacher stopped and looked at the painting she was working on. She heard him call several of the students who were still there to come and look at what she had done that day. Then she heard the teacher say, "If that girl would only wake up, she would become a really great artist." The next day she came to school earlier than usual. That was the beginning of a new life for her. She had been at the bottom of her class, but she graduated at the top of her class. Her teacher said to her, "You need have no hesitation in opening your own studio. You will succeed."

It was a happy experience for me to pray with her at the opening of her studio. Later she painted a small picture of the church of which I was the pastor at that time, and that picture now hangs on the wall of my home and is one of my precious possessions.

The truth is, there is something in every one of us that is good and needs to be expressed. As we express the good, the timidity in our lives is driven away.

You Need Not Be Afraid

The greatest trouble with trouble is to anticipate it with fear. We remember that Job said, "For the thing which I greatly feared is come upon me, and that which I was afraid of is come unto me" (Job 3:25). The first thing to do with your troubles is not to be afraid of them. One of the supreme teachings of the Scriptures is that if you have God, you do not need to be afraid. Over and over, people have quoted to themselves these beloved and familiar words, "Let not your heart be troubled: ye believe in God . . ." (John 14:1). As long as we have God, we do not need to be afraid.

Just a few nights ago, my ten-year-old grandson spent the night with me. We had been out and had a lovely dinner together. After we got back home we got out the checkerboard and played checkers for a while, and then we watched television. Finally it was time to go to bed. I live in a big house alone, so I have plenty of room. I said to my little grandson, "Here are three nice bedrooms; you may take your choice and sleep in any one of the three you like." He replied very firmly, "I am not going to sleep in any of these rooms. I am going to sleep with you." That little boy did not want to be alone, and as long as he was with his grandfather, he felt safe and secure.

Over and over I tell people they can sum up the Christian faith in three words: "God loves you." The important thing is to never forget that. So many times we quit thinking of God, and we concentrate on trouble, and we eventually feel separated from God. Then we need to remind ourselves of Saint Paul's wonderful declaration about trouble. Every so often, I read these marvelous and wonderful words:

> Who shall separate us from the love of Christ? shall tribulation, or distress, or persecution, or famine, or nakedness, or peril, or sword? As it is written, For thy sake we are killed all the day long; we are accounted as sheep for the slaughter. Nay, in all these things we are more than conquerors through him that loved us. For I am persuaded, that neither death, nor life, nor angels, nor principalities, nor powers, nor things present, nor things to come, Nor height, nor depth, nor any other creature, shall be able to separate us from the love of God, which is in Christ Jesus our Lord.
>
> Romans 8:35-39

I repeat, the first thing to do with your troubles is not to be afraid of them. I think I learned this best more than thirty years ago. I was living in Atlanta, Georgia, at that time, and one morning I was going to Rome, Georgia, to speak at noon. That evening, I was coming back down to Cartersville, Georgia, to preach at night. As I was dressing, I felt some pain in my back, but I was sure it would pass away. I mentioned it to my wife, and she insisted that I see a doctor before I left town, so really to please my wife, I phoned my doctor and got an appointment that morning. He was an especially good friend of mine, and I knew he would get me out very quickly. After feeling my back and my chest, he decided I needed to be x-rayed. As he was studying the results I was getting impatient because I was in a hurry to make my noon engagement. Then he said to me, "You are going to the hospital." I asked him what was wrong with me, and he told me that I had a spontaneous pneumothorax. I asked him what that is, and he explained that one of my lungs was losing air, and soon it would be completely flat, like a flat tire on a car. This was on Thursday morning, and I said to the doctor, "Of course, I will be able to preach next Sunday." He replied, "No, you will not preach next

Sunday, and you will not preach for several Sundays." Then in a very kind and loving way, this dear friend of mine said to me, "Charles, you may never preach again."

He explained that I did not have a disease, but that my lung had sprung a leak, and it could happen again any time I began to preach. I did go to the hospital, and I got along fine. After three weeks, I preached again in my pulpit. During that sermon I was very conscious of my back. I think I was wondering more about whether there was a pain developing there than I was concentrating on what I was saying. For some time after that, every time I spoke in public it was a really difficult experience.

One night God healed me. God did not heal my lung; the truth is, it had already been healed. What God healed was the trouble in my mind. As I lay in bed that particular night, suddenly it seemed that God's hand was upon my head, and it was as if He just reached into my mind and lifted out that fear. I felt relaxed, and I slept better that night than I had in some weeks. This was more than thirty years ago, and that trouble with my lung has never reoccurred. More importantly I have never been afraid that it would reoccur.

One of the dearest friends of my life was Ernest Rogers. His father and my father were ministers together in Georgia. They were close friends and later Ernest and I became just as close in our friendship. For many years he wrote a daily column for the *Atlanta Journal,* and I wrote a daily column for the *Atlanta Constitution.* Many times we had lunch together and would talk about many things. He told me about a period in his life when he "got off the track," but he came back in a great way. In thinking about his experience he wrote a poem that means much to me:

> Maybe I failed in the final drive
> When sinew and nerve and heart
> Had lost the urge and the will to strive
> And I played the loser's part.

But down on my trembling knees I fall
  Though others may look askance
To say a prayer to the Lord of All
  The God of another chance.

Those who have drunk from the bitter cup
  And tasted the dregs of defeat
May win again if lifted up
  And placed in the mercy seat.

Lord, I search through the darkling skies
  For a word or a sign or a glance
That brings new light to my dimming eyes
  From the God of another chance.

"Winner take all" is the way of the pack
  The losers must weep alone;
The way is hard if they struggle back
  To try it again on their own.

But there is hope for the winner's share
  For those who would advance
By lifting up abiding prayer
  To the God of another chance.

So down on my trembling knees I fall
  Though others may look askance
To say a prayer to the Lord of All
  The God of another chance.

My sister, Frances, was just eighteen months older than I. We grew up together and I loved and appreciated her through all of the years. She married Robert Chamberlain, and they built a house and lived very, very happily in Longmeadow, Massachusetts. There developed a pain in her back, and it was diagnosed as cancer. The doctors found that it had spread too far in her system to treat effectively. She died with a beautiful spirit, without fear and without resentment.

After she died, her husband, Bob, found a special letter in her dresser drawer. Among other things, she told him that she was enclosing with this letter a poem, and every so often she wanted him to read these words after she was gone. It is such a wonderful poem that I wish every person who has a loved one who is now dead would read this poem and live by it:

Poem for the Living

When I am dead,
Cry for me a little.
Think of me sometimes,
But not too much.
It is not good for you
Or your wife or your husband
Or your children
To allow your thoughts to dwell
Too long on the dead.
Think of me now and again
As I was in life
At some moment which it is pleasant to recall.
But not for long.
Leave me in peace
As I shall leave you, too, in peace.
While you live,
Let your thoughts be with the living.

THEODORA KROEBER

There Is a Time to Laugh

Never forget, the Bible tells us that there is "a time to laugh." The Bible says that there are times for other things, such as to weep, to mourn, to dance, to embrace, to get, to lose, to keep, to rend, to sew, be silent, to speak, to love, to hate, for war, for peace—each of these things are essential parts of life. But, somehow, I feel that we need to be reminded there is "a time to laugh" (Ecclesiastes 3:1–10).

In genuine laughter the mind flings open its doors and windows, and its dim and dusty corners are filled with air and sunshine. People who forget how to laugh are the ones who suffer the most. Some people are so painfully good that they had rather be right than be pleasant. That thought has been expressed by many persons many times and it is still the truth.

Instead we should have this attitude:

Then Laugh

Build for yourself a strong box,
    Fashion each part with care;
Fit it with hasp and padlock,
    Put all your troubles there.
Hide therein all your failures,
    And each bitter cup you quaff
Lock all your heartaches within it,
    Then sit on the lid and laugh.

Tell no one its contents;
    Never its secrets share
Drop in your cares and worries,
    Keep them forever there,
Hide them from sight so completely
    The world will never dream half.
Fasten the top down securely,
    Then sit on the lid and laugh.

BERTHA ADAMS BACKUS

Someone has well said, "God must have had a good sense of humor, else He could not have made monkeys, pelicans, and some of us." Laughter gives us a wholesome attitude toward our fellowman. When two people laugh together, there is a sense of belonging. Laughter carries with it a sympathy for others; it tends to remove suspicion, doubts, and antagonism. When we laugh together, we feel united, we are ready to forgive, we begin to love. People cannot hate each other while they are laughing.

It has been beautifully written:

> Laugh and the world laughs with you;
> Weep and you weep alone;
> For the sad old earth, must borrow its mirth,
> It has trouble enough of its own.
>
> Rejoice and men will seek you;
> Grieve and they turn and go;
> They want full measure of all your pleasure,
> But they do not want your woe.
>
> Be glad, and your friends are many;
> Be sad, and you lose them all;
> There are none to decline your nectar wine,
> But alone you must drink life's gall.
>
> ELLA WHEELER WILCOX

Laughter can help us over more difficult places than any other expression of mankind. There is a story of Jimmy Durante, whom many of us remember as a great American comic. He told of an experience when he was a boy. His mother bought him a Buster Brown suit with a large, flowing collar. On Sunday she made him wear it. He was very self-conscious and never wanted anybody to see him in that suit. If the other boys saw him, he would really be scorned. One day he caught sight of himself in a store window. As he looked at himself he began to laugh; as he was laughing along came the other boys. One asked, "What is so funny?" He replied, "Look, a guy dressed like a sissy, with a face like a horse." Soon they were all laughing. Then it dawned upon Jimmy Durante that as long as he could make people laugh, they would be safe with each other. So he spent his life making people laugh.

Jimmy Durante's "schnozzolla," his big, ugly nose, became his greatest asset. The truth is, we all have schnozzolas of some kind. In some way each one of us is ridiculous, if not in our faces, then in our characters or minds or habits. Instead of being ashamed of our schnozzollas, we need to begin to laugh. Really, only the one with the pure, clean conscience can enjoy the highest laughter. Only one who loves can know the real joy of laughter. Ultimately all genuine laughter depends on our trust in God, upon our sense of security.

Lynn Harold Huff, who was for many years the distinguished dean of Drew University, said these words:

> The man who takes the risk of believing in a universe ruled over by a Christ-like God finds all the founts of faith and joy playing in his spirit. Laughter is heritage while he can see the face of God in the face of Jesus. And the deepest and most beautiful mystery of the Christian religion is found at Calvary. For, if you can be sure there is a cross in the heart of God, you can be sure of laughter in the heart of man.

There is a story of a man who went in search of a flower called hearts ease. Upon every road he took, however, he found an obstacle blocking his progress. That obstacle was his brother's burden. At last in desperation he decided to lift that unwelcome obstacle, because he could continue his search in no other way. Then to his utter amazement, he found the lovely flower of hearts ease blooming under the burden he lifted. Even so, if we will lift someone's burden, we will find blooming in our very path the lovely flower of a cheerful heart.

The ultimate in living in the fourth dimension is joy in our hearts and laughter in our lives.